Greenhouse Gardening

By the Editors of Sunset Books and Sunset Magazine

LANE PUBLISHING CO. • MENLO PARK, CALIFORNIA

Foreword

Many changes have occurred in both the greenhouse structure and its uses, and this guide presents greenhouse gardening as it is today.

No longer is the greenhouse an expensive toy used only for growing a few prized blossoms. Today, inexpensive and easy-to-use plastics have greatly lowered the cost of greenhouses, placing them within reach of most gardeners. And this new breed of greenhouse gardener will try anything that grows—it is not at all uncommon to find tomatoes and cucumbers growing in the same greenhouse with specimen orchids and bromeliads.

Whether you're thinking of buying or building a greenhouse or expanding the usefulness of your present house, you will find in this book a comprehensive overview of the greenhouse structure and a practical guide to the many ways it can be utilized.

Edited by Kathryn L. Arthurs

Design and Artwork: Terrence Meagher

Cover: This gardener takes advantage of the greenhouse environment to get a head start on spring and summer gardening. Photograph by Ells Marugg.

Executive Editor, Sunset Books: David E. Clark

First Printing, March 1976

Contents

Greenhouses

– then and now

As soon as ancient man turned from nomadic hunting to agriculture, he saw the advantages of controlling his environment. If he could control the climate, a gardener could grow crops out of season and provide fresh fruits and vegetables when he needed them.

Archeological evidence points to the possibility that gardeners as far back as the Greeks and Romans achieved limited success in creating an indoor environment suited to growing various plants throughout the year. Documented attempts in the 17th century include the *orangeries* built in France to produce oranges and other citrus fruits for privileged royal palates. In other European countries, there were experiments with heated sheds and buildings containing expanses of glass set at varying angles to catch the rays of the sun. Whatever methods these greenhouse pioneers employed, they met with enough success that other gardeners

Conservatory of Flowers *in Golden Gate Park, San Francisco, is replica of Victorian conservatory at Kew Gardens, England.*

felt encouraged to continue the search for the perfect structure with a controlled climate suited to growing plants.

The Victorian era was the golden age of greenhouses. Architects applied new technology to greenhouse structures that let them use large, curved panes of glass held in place by thin metal frames. Improved heating systems were becoming less toxic to plant life.

The Victorians did everything in a big way, and their greenhouses were no exception—these elaborate structures were huge and sported high domes, towers, cupolas, numerous wings, and gingerbread decorations. Many of these glasshouses enclosed several acres, and they provided a perfect climate for growing the many exotic plant specimens that were zealously being collected from all parts of the British Empire. Curiously, these new improved greenhouses were rarely used for growing food crops.

Greenhouses in the Victorian tradition can still be found; the Conservatory of Flowers in San Francisco's Golden Gate Park, pictured on the opposite page, is a stunning example.

As technology improved, so did the greenhouse. Many established arboretums acquired large greenhouses to contain their growing collections of rare and exotic plants. And many individual gardeners, especially those living in harsh winter areas, found that a home greenhouse let them garden the year around.

Because of man's persistence, the greenhouse idea has advanced to our present-day structures of glass and metal, plastic and wood. Our current technology not only provides us with the proper climate controls for all types of greenhouse gardening, it also gives us complete automation: a well-equipped greenhouse can run for weeks without any human intervention. And modern man has brought us full circle—many northern European countries rely on large commercial greenhouses to provide them with fresh produce.

As to the future, the greenhouse idea may well be expanded to provide a controlled climate for people as well as plants.

Huge geodesic domes have been designed as models of controlled environments. R. Buckminster Fuller's dome constructed for Expo '67 in Montreal, Canada, was designed especially for people (see the photograph at lower right). These ideas could be applied to make colonization possible in very hostile climates, such as the Arctic, where normal human life would be impossible. Or, in the more distant future, controlled environments could be used for Earth colonies in outer space.

If some of these future possibilities for the greenhouse and its controlled environment idea sound far-fetched, just remember ancient man, who only wanted to stretch the growing season a little. How far we've come since then!

Azalea House *at Longwood Gardens, Kennett Square, Pennsylvania, is one of many display greenhouses. Here, a landscape complete with trees is totally under glass.*

Palm House, *another greenhouse located at Longwood Gardens, creates tropical atmosphere for palm trees, other exotic plants—a sharp contrast to wintry weather.*

Futuristic dome *houses an aviary, creates a totally controlled environment. Designed by R. Buckminster Fuller, this dome was U.S. Pavilion in Expo '67 held at Montreal.*

THE ANATOMY OF A GREENHOUSE

A greenhouse is a place of magic—a structure of glass and metal or plastic and wood that helps you grow plants as never before. To capture this magic, you will need to acquire the greenhouse that's just right for you and for the plants you want to grow.

In this first section, you look closely at the greenhouse structure broken down into its many parts. This in-depth look is to help you select the best style greenhouse, its location, the building materials that are best for your climate, and the equipment you'll need to create the greenhouse environment.

Each facet of the greenhouse structure will require that you make certain decisions; make them carefully, for they will determine both the possibilities and the limitations of your greenhouse gardening.

Cost will probably weigh heavily in many of these decisions. As with any purchase, making the best use of your investment is important. Look for materials and equipment that offer efficiency as well as economy.

Once all the decisions are made and the greenhouse is a reality, you can begin to discover the pleasure —and magic—of greenhouse gardening.

Garden work center *in side yard is perfect spot for this greenhouse. Coldframe and potting bench with storage below provide extra work space. Fence screens wood-and-glass greenhouse from garden view.*

Which shape? What size?

The type of greenhouse you select will depend on several factors: the amount of money you want to invest, the amount and location of the space you have available, the climate in which you live, and the plants you plan to grow. Since each of these factors is important, you should base your decision on the type of greenhouse that most closely fits your needs in all four respects.

The cost factor can be critical. Be forewarned—the cost of the greenhouse itself is only the beginning. You will also need to provide a foundation and/or flooring, utilities, and the various systems necessary to control the greenhouse climate, such as heating, cooling, and ventilation. Also be prepared for the cost of energy required to maintain the greenhouse climate throughout the year.

The other factors are discussed in more detail later: for site location information see pages 14-17; for the various building materials, pages 24-29; for climate considerations, page 17; for suggestions of plants, pages 64-91.

A houselike greenhouse

The word "greenhouse" conjures up for most people the image of an even-span structure. Conventional even-span greenhouses are symmetrical, house-shaped buildings with pitched roofs (see sketch below). Walls may be vertical or angled; they may be built entirely of glass or plastic, or the lower half of the wall may be constructed of a solid material such as brick or cement.

Because even-span greenhouses are usually built as detached structures, building codes differ greatly from one area to another: further information appears on page 14. The climate in your area and the codes will dictate whether or not you'll need a full foundation.

Advantages. 1) Even-span greenhouses admit the maximum available light. 2) The houselike shape allows for the most interior growing space. Glass-to-ground wall construction lets you grow shade-loving plants under the benches. 3) The popularity of this style ensures you the best selection of size and building materials, including prefabricated units. 4) The shape is easy to enlarge later if you decide you want more space.

Disadvantages. 1) Since even-span greenhouses are usually detached buildings, utilities must be provided. Depending on the distance from existing utilities, this can be a costly procedure. 2) Because of the relatively large size of an even-span

house, construction costs may be higher than for other types, especially the lean-to style. 3) This type greenhouse may take up a large area of your yard—a possible problem if you have a small lot. 4) You may find the distance from your house a nuisance, particularly during inclement weather. (This can be a drawback with any detached greenhouse.)

A lean-to look

By definition, a lean-to greenhouse "leans" against and shares a wall with another structure. The supporting structure is generally a house, but a lean-to greenhouse also can be affixed to a garage, shed, fence—any walled structure that can support it.

The most common lean-to greenhouse resembles one half of an even-span house (see sketch below). These lean-to structures utilize one large wall already in existence, cutting down on the initial building costs. Other style possibilities for a lean-to include one half of a Gothic arch, Quonset, or A-frame greenhouse.

Occasionally, an even-span greenhouse is constructed in lean-to fashion—connected at right angles to the supporting wall, with one of the short end walls attached. This type of joining permits twice as much growing space as the usual lean-to, with almost the same advantages. The building cost would probably be higher.

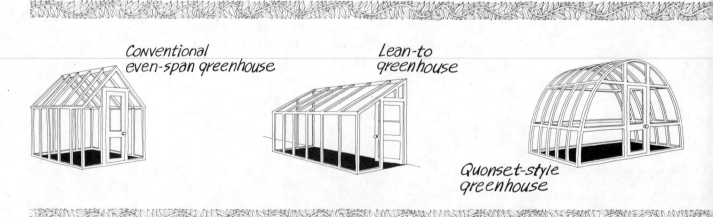

Conventional even-span greenhouse

Lean-to greenhouse

Quonset-style greenhouse

Lean-to greenhouses can be constructed with vertical or angled walls. Walls may be glass-to-ground, or the lower portion of the wall may be built of wood, brick, cement, or other solid materials. Glass-to-ground construction allows for more growing space inside the greenhouse.

Advantages. 1) A lean-to greenhouse shares a wall with another structure, usually a house. Since one greenhouse wall will be eliminated, cost of building materials and construction will be lower than for a detached structure. 2) The proximity to your house allows for easy utilities connections (water, electricity, gas). It also may allow you to extend the present house heating system into the greenhouse rather than purchase a separate system. 3) You may be able to channel into your house some of the solar heat created in the greenhouse. 4) The common wall permits access directly from the house to the greenhouse through that wall, making it very convenient for the gardener. 5) Since it's usually attached to the house, a lean-to greenhouse can double as a garden room. It may also create a pleasant view for the adjoining interior space. 6) If you are designing a new home, a lean-to greenhouse can become an integral part. Greenhouse units used as architectural elements are discussed on pages 22-23. 7) The supporting structure's wall space may be used for vining plants. These plants can be grown attached directly to the wall.

Disadvantages. 1) Since one greenhouse wall has been eliminated, the amount of growing space will be reduced. Available light will also be lessened because of limited exposure. If the lower half of the greenhouse wall is constructed from solid building materials, both light and growing space will be limited even more. 2) The addition of a lean-to greenhouse could be out of keeping with the style and landscape of your home. If you feel such a structure would be visually jarring, yet a lean-to is still the best choice for your purposes, consult an architect, landscape architect, or structural designer for advice. 3) Because of house design and location, the choice of possible supporting walls for a lean-to structure could be limited to a location with poor light, such as a north exposure. If this is a problem, consider installing artificial lights or growing only plants that tolerate lower light levels. 4) Local building codes may be stricter regarding lean-to greenhouses if they are considered house additions. Before investing time and money, become familiar with building codes and regulations that would pertain to your situation. Building codes are discussed in more detail on page 14. 5) Because of the proximity of greenhouse and home, the unpleasant odors from fertilizing plants and spraying for diseases or pests can permeate your home. 6) Lean-to greenhouses are difficult to expand or add on to because of their design and limited location possibilities.

The humble Quonset

A Quonset-shaped greenhouse is a do-it-yourselfer's dream. These structures are easy to build from inexpensive, easy-to-manipulate materials. Many are framed with PVC (polyvinyl chloride) plastic pipe or wood, then covered with rigid or soft plastics. (These building materials are discussed on pages 24-29.) If you plan to build a Quonset-style greenhouse, ask your local supplier about the available sizes of these building materials and, if possible, design your greenhouse accordingly. Be sure to plan for adequate ventilation.

To find building materials in your area, look in the Yellow Pages of your telephone directory under "Greenhouse Equipment and Supplies," "Plastics," or "Building Materials." A few phone calls should locate the materials you will need.

Advantages. 1) A Quonset-shaped greenhouse is relatively easy for the average homeowner to construct. 2) Inexpensive building materials coupled with low construction costs may allow you to build a larger greenhouse than you could otherwise afford.

Disadvantages. 1) The Quonset shape makes these greenhouses hard to ventilate. This may require more than average equipment and more frequent checks by the owner. 2) If you use a soft plastic covering, be prepared to repair and replace it periodically. Be sure to plan for these expenses in your overall maintenance costs.

A-frames are possible

Its ability to shed snow easily and its low-cost construction make the "A" shape a popular design for mountain cabins. The same reasoning applies to greenhouses, and if snow is a problem in your area, an A-frame greenhouse may be the answer.

In heavy snow areas, a large snow buildup tends to form along the lower part of the structure. That buildup may create unequal lateral forces, caving in the roof or pushing in the side walls. A good precaution is to place the A-frame

A-frame greenhouse

Even-span greenhouse with angled walls

Geodesic dome greenhouse

on top of a solid wall (see photograph on page 11).
This solution also gives you more head room and growing
space, making the A-frame a more usable greenhouse.

Advantages. 1) Since there are only two walls—angled
together to form the roof—less building material is normally
needed. This should keep construction costs down. 2) The
A-frame is an interesting shape in the garden. 3) The roof
shape repels rain and snow easily. 4) This style greenhouse
is easy for the homeowner to construct.

Disadvantages. 1) The overhead growing space is much
smaller because of the greenhouse shape. 2) Floor space at the
sides is difficult for most gardeners to reach. 3) The roof
peak traps heat at the top; good ventilation and heat
circulation equipment will be needed. 4) The gardener
will have limited head space.

The Gothic arch soars

This greenhouse compares with the A-frame house in shape
and design (see photos on page 11). It too is hard to ventilate,
but its utilization of interior space is far superior.

Gothic arch greenhouses are easy to find in the form of
inexpensive prefabricated kits, or you can build one yourself
from scratch.

Conventional, even-span *greenhouse has fiberglass
roof, glass walls. Whitewash covers glass during summer
to provide shading, protect plants from sunburn.*

Glass front *of even-span greenhouse gives
pleasant view of garden area. Width of house
allows space for benches in center as well
as next to walls.*

Curved glass lean-to *has stucco foundation wall up to bench level, helping to blend green-house section with house. Greenhouse is used to start vegetables; plants are trans-planted to garden in foreground.*

Angled lean-to *of metal and glass rests on concrete block foundation wall. Wooden slat blinds roll down when shading is needed. Glass shelves on window wall increase growing space.*

Gothic arch house *has snap-together plastic frame covered with soft plastic; can be moved from place to place. Benches are corrugated fiberglass.*

Metal frame greenhouse *combines Gothic arch and Quonset styles. Metal clips hold easy-to-replace glass panes for walls, roof.*

A-frame structure *was placed on foundation wall of brick to increase growing space, head room. Green-house is of fiberglass with wood and metal frame. Top vent keeps hot air from accumulating at roof peak.*

A futuristic geodesic dome

A dome-shaped greenhouse has the look of the future. It will add a special point of interest to your garden without the usual utilitarian look of many greenhouses. This shape is called a geodesic (or geodetic) dome because the framework consists of geometric shapes, usually triangles, put together.

Advantages. 1) Inside, a dome greenhouse gives a sense of great space and airiness. 2) Dome-shaped greenhouses fall into the inexpensive category, along with the Quonset, A-frame, and Gothic arch houses.

Disadvantages. 1) Ventilation is difficult in a dome. 2) Benches for plants must be curved around the sides of the dome. Therefore, they are difficult to build and brace. 3) Overhead and bench growing space will be limited by the inward curve of the walls.

Put a greenhouse in your window

If space is a problem, or if you'd like to try greenhouse gardening before investing in a large structure, a window-size greenhouse may be the answer. Manufactured units fit over most standard window openings, making installation easy. And they require little additional equipment. The only problem is likely to be the quick realization that greenhouse gardening is too enjoyable to be confined to your window; your hobby requires more space. Some window greenhouses are illustrated at right and below.

Advantages. 1) Window greenhouses are inexpensive to build or purchase. 2) Prefabricated units come in standard window sizes. The various components can be altered if necessary to fit odd-size openings. 3) The window greenhouse can tap the room heat already provided; no special heating system will be needed. 4) Flowers and foliage plants at the window will create a pleasant view from both inside and outside.

Disadvantages. 1) Growing space is very limited. 2) Most window greenhouses open directly into the adjoining room, making it difficult to create a special greenhouse climate. 3) A window greenhouse contains such a small volume of air that the interior can heat rapidly to stifling heights. You will need to be constantly alert to the ventilating needs or purchase an automatic system. 5) Since a window greenhouse protrudes from the house wall, it may be difficult to seal it completely from air or water leaks.

Light, airy appearance *of in-the-round greenhouse is achieved with 1 by 4s and glass. Foundation wall and frame are of wood; walls are glass.*

Window-size *greenhouse has top that opens for ventilation.*

Seen *from inside, it adds dimension to room. Drapes can close it off.*

Window bay *doubles as greenhouse (above) off kitchen.* **Right:** *Design accents house architecture. Architect: Weldon Jean Skirvin.*

If you outgrow your greenhouse...

Many greenhouse gardeners eventually find that they need more growing space than their present houses can provide. One quick way to gain space is to install a coldframe or a hotbed adjacent to the greenhouse area, but these devices have limited uses and will serve only as stop gap measures (see pages 42-43 for more information on coldframes and hotbeds).

One way to gain space is to build a second greenhouse, but the best method of gaining growing space is to expand your present house. Some greenhouse styles, such as the geodesic dome, defy addition unless you alter their basic shape. Luckily, most other styles allow for easy expansion.

If your present greenhouse has a square or rectangular base, remove one wall—usually one of the shorter ones—and attach the new greenhouse area at that point. Most prefabricated models have stock components that make these additions easy.

Another method of expanding a rectangular house is to remove a long side wall and join a second house at that point, keeping the wall open. (You may need a gutter to handle water runoff.) An example of this type addition is pictured at right.

You can leave the adjoining wall intact, installing a door in it for access from one greenhouse to the other. This type of addition gives you two separate greenhouse environments that you can operate at different temperatures; you can have both a cool house and a warm one at the same time. The uses of cool and warm greenhouses are discussed on pages 82-86.

Lean-to greenhouses can be extended at either end, up to the length of the supporting wall. They can also function as two separate houses if the connecting wall is retained.

Be sure to check your local building codes—greenhouse expansion may require a new permit. Also, examine your present facilities for heating, water, electricity, ventilation, and any other system you want extended into the addition. Will your present system adequately handle the new greenhouse or will you need more equipment? Your greenhouse supplier is a good source of information regarding equipment and systems capacities.

Placed side by side, *these two even-span greenhouses (above) were connected to satisfy need for growing space.* **Left:** *Side walls were removed so both houses share the same climate equipment. Hanging plants stretch space.*

Second lean-to section *was placed next to original greenhouse when extra space was needed for starting cuttings, repotting. Temperatures can be kept at different levels in each section. Door allows for easy access.*

Coldframe *placed next to lean-to greenhouse provides additional space for growing seedlings. Lid opens for ventilation, added light.*

Zero in on the right site

Choosing the best site for your greenhouse may not be as easy as it sounds. The ideal location provides good daily light throughout the year, adheres to relevant building codes, protects the greenhouse from chronic weather problems like strong winds and heavy snow and rainfall, gives plants optimum growing conditions, lets the gardener work conveniently the year around, and presents the most pleasant appearance possible in your landscape. You may also want additional land left for future expansion of your greenhouse.

Such ideal locations are few and far between, but, with some compromises, most gardeners can find a suitable spot. With this ideal in mind, let's explore your situation to find the best possible location.

What you can and can't build

Many of the obstacles you'll encounter in finding space for a greenhouse will be out of your control: building codes, the amount of land you have available, obstructions—such as trees or buildings—located off your property that block light, and the amount of money you can spend. Since you can do little to change these situations, consider all your possible options carefully. You may find that some of the "obstacles" can work in your favor.

Building codes can be sticky

Most building construction and land use, including a hobby greenhouse, is regulated by local building codes. Local codes are based on regional codes, which are periodically updated by building officials. Your area may also have state regulations that can apply to your situation.

A phone call or visit to your local building permit office will inform you of the rules that deal with constructing a greenhouse on your property. Some areas will be virtually free of restrictions; other areas will follow very strict codes— one greenhouse owner in California needed to file an Environmental Impact Study before receiving a permit. Most people, though, encounter only moderate local restrictions regarding greenhouse construction.

To obtain a building permit in most areas, start by taking accurate plot and greenhouse placement plans to your building department. An inspector can tell whether or not your plans violate the code and can usually recommend changes to bring them into conformity.

If your plans do not conform to the code, don't despair— in many local building departments the person in charge has the power to authorize any code modifications you may need. Failing this, you have the alternatives to legally attempt to appeal the restrictive provisions (a time-consuming venture) or to proceed without the knowledge and approval of the building department (which can be risky). Be aware of the penalties involved before you ignore the code; you may pay a heavy fine or be forced to have the greenhouse removed or rebuilt to meet the code standards.

If it's a zoning ordinance hindering you (zoning ordinances regulate land use such as building height limitations, required distance between structures and property lines, and the percentage of a lot that can be covered with structures), you can apply for a variance. A variance also requires that you file a plot plan showing existing structures and the details of your proposed change or addition. If the variance

is minor, the zoning officer may grant it; this is subject to certification by the governing body and is called an administrative variance. If the variance calls for substantial changes, it must go before a board—usually a time-consuming procedure; check with your local department for the exact process to follow. Should the board refuse your request, you can appeal further to the council or board of supervisors, but their decision is final.

Many people find themselves frustrated by seemingly unreasonable building regulations. It helps if you keep in mind that building codes and zoning ordinances are meant as protective measures for the general public.

The problem of space

Most of us have limited amounts of land to devote to a greenhouse, and local building codes may limit the possibilities even more (see at left and above for information on building codes and zoning ordinances). You will need a location that can handle the size of the greenhouse you've selected and provide the necessary sunlight.

If your available land is very limited, remember that lean-to greenhouses are great space savers.

Incorporating part of a side yard area into a greenhouse makes use of space that often is wasted or used only to conceal utility storage. The photographs at top on the next page show one ingenious gardener's small-space house designed for a side yard area.

Greenhouse gardeners who live in apartments or condominiums might consider enclosing a porch or balcony. One such greenhouse is pictured at center on the next page; this house was constructed so it can be removed if the owner decides to move.

If space is no problem, try to keep your greenhouse close enough to the house to be convenient for you. Daily watering can become a chore during winter months or other periods of miserable weather if you have to wade through snow or rain puddles to reach the greenhouse.

Will the light be blocked?

Anything that blocks sunlight from reaching your greenhouse interior that you cannot (or will not) control or change is defined as a light obstruction. Houses and other structures on someone else's property; a hill or slope; trees or hedges owned by a neighbor; trees or shrubs on your own property that you prefer to keep—all would fit this criteria. Keep in mind that the ideal location for a greenhouse would

Side yard greenhouse *with fences on three sides (left) has fiberglass roof, soft plastic attached to slat-frame front wall. Fences double as growing space for climbing plants, hangers.* **Above:** *Small space inside is well used. Shade-loving plants, seedlings are placed under benches.*

Enclosed balcony *forms greenhouse in condominium (right). Sliding glass doors, drapes can close it off.* **Far right:** *Benches run length of room, provide ample growing space. Benches, window wall can be dismantled if owner moves.*

Hillside greenhouse *cuts into slope. Retaining walls and plants help to blend large structure into surroundings. Fiberglass roof, aluminum shading on walls filter sunlight. Covered entry forms sitting area.*

be free of these obstructions. However, finding a location completely free of obstacles will be practically impossible for most gardeners, especially those living in urban or suburban areas.

The location of these obstacles is very important. Obstructions located on the north side of the greenhouse will not affect light and can be ignored. Those located to the south and east of the greenhouse are most detrimental since they block the main concentration of sunlight. Obstacles to the west of the greenhouse are usually tolerable since they block the later rays of sun which are hotter and can damage plants.

The seasons have an effect on light as well. The winter sun moves in a lower position across the sky than the summer sun and may cause shadows created by obstacles located at a greater distance. This can be a major problem because the winter sun is much weaker, is frequently blocked by clouds or fog, and is present a shorter length of time each day.

Deciduous trees and shrubs that block sunlight can be beneficial. During the spring and summer, their shadows can serve as a screen, keeping the strong sunlight from scorching plants. During the fall and winter, these trees and shrubs lose their leaves, letting the weaker winter sun reach the greenhouse.

One way to test a site is to plot out the dimensions of the greenhouse with rope or wooden strips. Watch this outline for a day or two to see if any major shadows fall into it. If there is serious light blockage, maybe you should look for another location. If this is the only possible greenhouse site on your property, consider installing artificial lights. Still another solution would be to grow shade-loving plants.

Dollars and cents

While the actual cost of the greenhouse itself shouldn't affect your choice of locations, some of the other necessary expenses may have a bearing on the overall cost. The size of the greenhouse and its construction costs, the utilities connections, and the energy costs for maintaining the greenhouse environment should be considered before you finalize the site. One location could prove much more costly than another.

The larger the greenhouse structure, the higher construction costs will be. And if the location is hard to reach, the cost can go even higher. Try to choose a spot that will be convenient for delivery trucks and workmen if you will need them. Also, if your site needs to be leveled or excavated for a foundation, it should be accessible to the proper equipment.

New utilities connections will be more expensive if the greenhouse site is some distance away from your present hookups. This is a one-time cost, but the longer the connecting lines are, the more difficult and costly repairs will be.

How location affects plants

The location you choose for your greenhouse can have a profound effect on the plants you will grow. Greenhouse plants depend on you to provide their light and climate. You can even control the seasons by artificially shortening or lengthening the days. Since the purpose of your greenhouse is to grow plants, choose its location with the amount of available light it provides as the top priority.

Team up with the sun

Most plants will use the maximum amount of sunlight you can provide, and providing this light should be one of your main objectives in selecting a location. The positioning of the greenhouse within the chosen location is also important—but not vital.

Many experts feel a greenhouse should be placed so that the ridge line or axis runs north-south; then only one of the short ends will face north. This position is considered the best to provide maximum light for the greenhouse. Others feel an east-west ridge line is preferable, but in this position one of the long sides will receive north light, limiting you to shade-loving plants. Unfortunately, many people are faced with space problems that make these debates academic. Luckily, the newer greenhouse models are engineered to provide optimum light regardless of the facing by using large

Sunken greenhouse protects plants from both hot and cold weather (above). Corrugated fiberglass roof provides ample light. **Right:** *Plants sit on benches, under benches, even hang from rafters.*

Metal-and-glass lean-to was adapted to blend with house architecture. Flowering vine helps hide structural lines. Lower half of wall has façade like nearby fence and house wall.

glass or plastic panels and less framework than most older models. If you do have a great deal of space, consider facing your greenhouse so the maximum amount of light is available.

The best facing for a lean-to greenhouse would be with the long wall to the south or southeast; this facing permits the best and longest amount of light to reach the house. However, if this is impossible for your situation choose the best available location and compensate for the light loss.

If your greenhouse location can't provide enough light for the plants you want to grow, one way to solve the problem is to install artificial lighting. Almost all plants will grow and flower under artificial lights; see page 37 for further information. The necessary equipment and the energy required to operate it will be an added expense, but your light problem will be gone.

Another way to compensate for inadequate light would be to grow shade-loving plants in your greenhouse. Many plants, such as ferns and begonias, prefer strong but sunless light; these plants will do well in a north facing house or in a greenhouse where much of the sunlight is obstructed.

Come to grips with your climate

Many regions have such chronic weather problems as heavy rain or snow or strong winds. (Severe summer heat can also be a problem, but this is best handled with a cooling system, pages 33-34, and shading, pages 38-39.) A greenhouse in a location that is sheltered from these weather problems will be more economical to run and less likely to be damaged during storms.

Heavy rains may cause drainage problems in and around a greenhouse. To avoid standing water, choose a spot on high, well-drained ground or provide a drainage system before the house is erected. If really heavy rains frequently occur in your area, you may need a gutter system on the eaves of the greenhouse to control the runoff.

Snow is usually no problem as long as you provide adequate insulation and heating. Avoid placing your greenhouse in a low spot or a sheltered area where snowdrifts could build up.

If sleet and hail are problems, a hard plastic roof is recommended rather than glass or soft plastic, since hard plastic panels are less likely to shatter.

Strong winds can be a real problem. In cold weather, winds blowing over a greenhouse can rob it of its interior heat, escalating energy costs. Windbreaks are your most effective weapon.

A windbreak is a structure or other obstacle that "breaks" up the force of the wind. Specially planted trees or shrubs or openwork fences will all serve admirably. Wind is like water—it flows in a steady stream; a solid barrier, such as a dense hedge or an airtight fence, forces the flow up and over it, allowing the wind to come crashing down in a wave. An openwork windbreak lets the wind blow through it in an erratic manner, actually lessening the wind's force.

Remember that a windbreak also can obstruct light. Try to locate your windbreak where it will block the least amount of sunlight.

Tiny greenhouse *off garage (below) is perfect for owner's needs. Materials are salvaged windows, scrap house siding.* **Right:** *House is used to revive house plants, protect tender plants from frost, start plants from cuttings.*

Should you buy or build one?

Acquiring a greenhouse can be done in any of several ways. Some prospective owners prefer the convenience of buying a professionally engineered, prefabricated model; others like the challenge of building their own; a few may look for a used greenhouse to buy and refurbish; people faced with a problem situation may seek the advice of an architect or designer. Whichever methods you may be considering, you should base your decision on the amount of free time you can devote to the project, the sum of money you want to invest, and the kinds of skills you possess.

If buying is the answer...

The decision to buy a greenhouse—as opposed to building one from scratch—is probably based on several factors: reputable greenhouse manufacturers carry well-designed and engineered units in a wide range of prices; prefabricated models are relatively easy to assemble in a short time; many greenhouse suppliers offer the necessary equipment or will order it for you.

You may have additional reasons for preferring the convenience of purchasing a greenhouse, such as a particular design or type of building material that would be difficult to duplicate. Whatever your reasons, buying a greenhouse will provide you with a reliable structure that can be completely operative in a relatively short time.

Choice 1: Pick up a prefab

Prefabricated greenhouses run the gamut from small, inexpensive, soft-plastic-and-wood structures; through standard-size units covered with hard plastic, glass, or a combination of the two; to the elegant houses made of curved glass and metal frames. Whatever your particular need, you should be able to find a prefabricated greenhouse that will fill it. In selecting the best greenhouse for your purposes, look for building materials that will be best suited to your climate, a style that will blend into your landscape, and the largest amount of growing space within your price range.

Your first step should be to acquaint yourself with the market. Get catalogues from as many greenhouse manufacturers as possible. (You will find a partial list of manufacturers on page 95.) As with any other purchase, it's a good idea to see several models before you select one. By all means find time to see the model you decide to buy and arrive at a very clear understanding of just what you will receive from the manufacturer and what it will cost. The package price of most kits usually does not include foundation, heaters, instruments, wiring, lights, plumbing, sink, or the delivery of the utilities to the site. The actual cost of the greenhouse will depend on the building materials you select, the size of the unit, and any shipping costs that apply.

It's also a good idea to purchase the necessary equipment at the same time you order the greenhouse (see pages 30-39 for further information). Most manufacturers supply equipment and can advise you of the sizes and types of systems your particular model requires.

Most people who are at all handy have little or no difficulty with fitting or assembling wood-and-glass or wood-and-hard-plastic conventional greenhouses. They usually find these units go together quickly and easily. Less expensive houses made of soft plastic and wood or fiberboard may be more difficult to assemble. Fitting and taping or attaching the soft plastic can be frustrating; nailing together inexpensive frames and doors may also prove difficult. Be sure to ask your greenhouse manufacturer just how much assembling and skill your particular greenhouse kit will require.

Once properly assembled, all prefabricated units become functioning greenhouses; the main difference between these various greenhouses will be longevity. You should try to keep in mind when you select a prefabricated unit that less permanent building materials, while less costly in the beginning, will require more maintenance and may require frequent replacement.

Concealed-from-view greenhouse was built between patio windbreak, retaining wall (right). Brick walkway adds rustic charm. **Above:** *Greenhouse is used for ferns, house plants; protects other plants from frost. Designer: Richard B. Morrall.*

Choice 2: Work with an architect

Only a small percentage of greenhouses are designed by architects, landscape architects, or designers. But many of the specially designed structures are filled with innovative ideas. Some architects incorporate prefabricated greenhouse sections or units into their designs (see pages 22-23); others create interesting new structures, either attached to a house or separate, that complement both the house and its surroundings.

Frequently, architects design the greenhouse so it can serve as family living space. As long as the proper equipment is installed, your growing space can easily double as a garden room, sitting room, or entertaining area.

There are several advantages in using an architect or designer. These professionals are trained to deal with structural problems and provide new or unusual solutions. They are familiar with local building codes and are accustomed to working with difficult spaces. Architects design structures, including greenhouses, with the surroundings in mind; these greenhouses will often echo the style of a home and blend into or serve as an accent for the landscape, eliminating the starkly utilitarian look that many greenhouse gardeners fear. Architects also may suggest new ideas for using space inside the house.

If you decide to use an architect or designer, you can hire that person as a consultant for working out specific problems or have him or her actually design the greenhouse and oversee its construction. Be sure the architect or designer you choose is well versed in the needs of growing plants and the various systems your greenhouse should contain.

Choice 3: Go the second hand route

Occasionally an interested buyer can find a used greenhouse that will fill his need. And a good secondhand greenhouse will probably be much less expensive than a new one. Possible sources include greenhouse gardeners who are buying larger greenhouses and people uninterested in gardening who purchase property that contains a greenhouse.

One way to locate a secondhand house is to advertise. If your area has a local shopper's newspaper, use it, or inquire through the classified section of your regular newspaper. At the present time, secondhand greenhouses are not common items, so you will need to be patient. Remember, too, that it's unlikely you'll find the exact greenhouse you'd like; be prepared to make a few compromises.

A used greenhouse will probably require some repairs, especially if it has been vacant for a time. Be sure the structure is stable and that the walls are relatively airtight. Check all the equipment very carefully before you begin to use it. Once you have the used greenhouse situated and refurbished, it should function as well as any other greenhouse.

Living room extension, *this greenhouse (left) provides good working space and a pleasant view from house. Covered plastic cans store ingredients for potting mix. Glass doors, tall windows blend with house architecture.*
Above: *Bench contains layer of pebbles; when wet, pebbles help provide humidity. Propagation tray at right has heating coils at base for starting cuttings, seeds. Architect: Marvin F. Damman.*

So you like to build...

Building your own greenhouse can be a satisfying experience—it may also prove frustrating. A do-it-yourselfer will probably find that building a greenhouse will be less expensive than buying a prefabricated house: you can use inexpensive standard-size building materials; you can incorporate salvaged items or discontinued products such as odd-size windows or doors into the design; and your labor is free.

Doing it yourself allows you to make your greenhouse any size you want; you aren't bound by the manufacturers' "standard sizes." You are free to use new materials and innovative designs. You will also be able to customize the interior space to fit your needs. If the greenhouse gardener is only five feet tall, for example, you may find that lowering the benches several inches will be helpful.

Time is an important factor. Though your labor is free, how much free time can you devote to the project? Also, do you have all the building skills required? Some jobs, such as installing the plumbing or electricity, are best left to professionals. You may also find that contracting out a few of the other more difficult jobs—pouring a concrete floor or welding together a metal frame—can expedite the project.

You will probably need a building permit to erect your own greenhouse. Follow the procedures required by your local building office; see page 14 for further information.

Once the construction is completed and all the systems are functioning, most greenhouse gardeners who opted for building their own are pleased with the results. And they have the satisfaction of knowing they did it themselves.

Collecting design ideas

Greenhouse blueprints can be of your own making or you can use published plans of engineered and time-tested houses.

If you decide to design your own greenhouse, you should be aware of how a well-planned house functions. It might be a good idea to have your final drawings checked by an architect, designer, or greenhouse manufacturer or supplier before you begin building. Once the house is up, any problem areas or mistakes will be difficult to remedy.

Published plans for all types of greenhouse structures are readily available; most require a small fee. Many state universities or university extension services offer greenhouse plans utilizing innovative designs and new building materials. A few of these publications are listed below:

A Simple Rigid Frame Greenhouse for Home Gardeners, by J. W. Coutier and J. O. Curtis. Cooperative Extension Service, Circular 880, University of Illinois, College of Agriculture, Urbana, IL 61801.

Home Greenhouses for Year-round Gardening Pleasure, by J. W. Coutier and J. O. Curtis. Cooperative Extension Service, Circular 879, University of Illinois, College of Agriculture, Urbana, IL 61801.

Electric Heating of Hotbeds, by the U.S. Department of Agriculture. Leaflet 445, Washington, DC 20250.

Garden and Patio Building Book, by the Editors of Sunset Books. Lane Publishing Co., Menlo Park, CA 94025.

Information on Greenhouse Plans, by Virginia Polytechnic Institute. Blacksburg, VA 24060.

List of Sources of Information on Greenhouses, by the U.S. Department of Agriculture. Correspondence Aid 34-134, Washington, DC 20250.

New Shapes of Hobby Greenhouses, by R. C. Liu, W. A. Bailey, H. H. Klueter, and D. T. Krizek. U.S. Department of Agriculture, ASAE Paper 68-925, Phyto-Engineering Laboratory, Beltsville, MD 20705.

Small Plastic Greenhouses, by the U.S. Department of Agriculture. Leaflet 2003, University of California, Berkeley, CA 94720.

Construction tips

Building a greenhouse is much like building any other houselike structure. You should work from the ground up and from the outside in, starting with preparation of the site and finishing with completion of the interior details of the greenhouse.

Once your design is finalized and you've acquired any necessary building permits, you can start buying the building

Lean-to greenhouse *converts to a shade house during late spring, summer, early fall. Roof covering at peak comes off for ventilation. During winter it protects tender plants from frost. House wall holds narrow plant shelves.*

materials you'll need. Try to purchase all these materials at the same time; running out of something midway in the construction can be frustrating, especially if the item has to be ordered and a delay results.

Your initial task will be preparing the greenhouse site. When the ground is leveled, you can put in the foundation and a drainage system, if needed. Utilities hookups and plumbing can be installed at the same time. If portions of the work will be done by contractors, find out from them at what point in the construction their particular project should be done; then schedule your time accordingly.

If you're going to pour a concrete floor, try to do it before the walls are up. Once the site is ready, you can begin the actual construction of the greenhouse.

A-frame mini-greenhouse *has lift-off side panels for easy access, ventilation. Heating cables are under soil in bench to provide heat, help start flats of cuttings. Water pipes along bench edge have mist nozzles to help provide humidity.*

Pint-size greenhouse *has window walls (left). Peaked roof gives structure ample head room once gardener is inside. Walls hold three tiers of plant shelves.* **Above:** *Frame is of 2 by 4s with salvaged windows nailed into place. Floor is brick set into sand. During winter peaked roof holds hanging baskets of fuchsias, geraniums, protecting them from frost.*

These people live in glass houses

Curved glass greenhouse sections *form one wall and ceiling of second-floor guest room, master bedroom, two-story living room, and first-floor dining room. Architect: Peter Behn.*

Former deck *is now enclosed with two slant-wall greenhouse sections, creating new room just off master bedroom. Bronze-tinted, heat retardant glass keeps temperatures down. Designer: Jack Comey.*

Add a greenhouse section to a house and the result is like a hybrid between a greenhouse and a patio—a place combining both house and garden.

Architects, who incorporate greenhouse sections into many homes, both new and old, know that prefabricated sections dramatically enhance a home while creating a place in which to relax. Unlike a greenhouse, this special glass room has people as its focal point. Plants aren't a necessity, though they can flourish and provide a soothing background.

The greenhouse sections shown here are prefabricated modules available from greenhouse dealers. Since many garden rooms are added to finished homes, the adaptability and wide choice of module styles are especially welcome. You should, of course, select the site for your new room before choosing the sections.

Two locations are favored for greenhouse sections that will contain many plants: one is at ground level against a sunny wall; the other is on an upper level enclosing an existing porch or balcony. In very hot areas, a north-facing location is best—there's plenty of light but less heat. Southern, eastern, and western exposures are better in coastal and other cool areas and are suitable also in hot areas if certain precautions are taken. It's possible to modify the amounts of heat and light entering your greenhouse section by coating the walls and roof with a heat reflecting material such as whitewash, covering them with heat reflecting transparent film, putting up shades, and ventilating the room. Even if you live in the desert and have a west-facing porch or balcony, you can still construct a garden room— it just takes a little more work.

Greenhouse sections are usually available in 24, 30, and 36-inch-wide glass modules in several shapes and heights. Most people use sections that have an aluminum framework, but some use those with a wooden frame (usually treated redwood; see pages 26-27) . Metal frames should require less maintenance and are more weatherproof; they are also more expensive.

Once ordered, the individual greenhouse parts will be delivered to the site and then assembled. Assembly is usually uncomplicated and can be done by an accomplished handyman. Most suppliers offer installation service; they'll quote you prices on request.

Though sections with curved walls are often chosen for their good looks, the slant and straight-wall sections are generally more leak resistant. Both types can be ordered with tempered, heat-retardant, or wired glass, often required by local building codes.

Roll-up vinyl or aluminum slat shades are frequently used over the exterior to cut down on heat absorption and glare. Motorized lifters actuated by a thermostat are available; these automatically open the overhead ventilating windows once a preselected temperature is reached, so you don't walk into an ovenlike room. This system isn't foolproof, though—the windows can open when it's raining.

The biggest challenge in installing a greenhouse section is preventing leaks. Flashing should always overlap the section where it joins an existing structure. When installing the glass, use silicone caulking at all joints.

Separate your glass room from the rest of the house; large doors—sliding or accordion pleated types—are the most versatile. Installed between the house and your new room, the doors can be opened wide so the greenhouse section and the room to which it's joined are one. Installed on an outer wall of the greenhouse section, large doors can make an outside patio part of the glass room. They also allow you to move furniture and large plants in and out more easily.

Flooring is another important feature. If you decide to have plants in the greenhouse section, the floor should be resistant to spilled water, dirt, and sun damage. Several choices are available: brick, ceramic tile, and linoleum are practical; so are cork tiles or wood if they are sealed with polyurethane varnish; and there are others.

Heating shouldn't be forgotten, either. The attention you give it will depend on the climate in your area. In most places, heating is necessary at some time of year. Extending your central heating system into the greenhouse section is the easiest method in the long run—once you set the thermostat, the selected temperature will be maintained. If your present heating system can't handle the additional load, you might consider a portable heater.

Furniture, a finishing touch, blends better if it's made of natural materials, whose colors and textures go well with plants. Wicker, wood, cane, and bamboo are examples of pleasing materials. Other types of garden furniture, such as wrought iron or aluminum, will fit in if they aren't too ornate. If you plan to have fabric-covered chair seats or cushions, choose a material that won't be damaged by water or sunlight.

To locate greenhouse section suppliers, look in the Yellow Pages under "Greenhouse Builders" or check the partial list on page 95. Before ordering, be sure you understand the building code specifications for your area, and remember to get a permit. Then add a section—or two —and we'll bet it becomes the most enjoyable room in your home.

Second-story sitting room *doubles as studio and greenhouse; roof and two end walls are commercial glass-and-metal greenhouse material. Roof panels are painted white in summer to control heat.*

Dramatic roofline *is created by two curved glass greenhouse sections. Rooftop room provides pleasant habitat for plants and an entertaining area with a view. Architect: Stuart Goforth.*

Putting it all together

The various parts that make up the greenhouse structure—foundation, frame, walls, roof, and floor—when put together create a shell designed to contain an environment for growing plants. Each of these parts, in some form, is necessary to the greenhouse structure.

The form each part takes is a matter of choice. Many of the new building materials being used in greenhouses—soft plastic coverings and PVC pipe frames, to name just two—are less permanent than the traditional glass and metal. Depending on your climate, your finances, and the functions you expect your greenhouse to perform, you can build either a permanent or a temporary greenhouse.

Foundation facts

Don't be like the foolish man who built his house upon the sand; by all means, provide a firm foundation for your greenhouse. This doesn't mean, though, that every greenhouse requires a complete foundation of concrete or brick. You may need only footings or posts to anchor the structure. A foundation is usually constructed below or at ground level, and it forms the base upon which the greenhouse rests.

Manufacturers of prefabricated greenhouses rarely include the foundation in their kits, but they will usually recommend specifications. The cost will depend on the type of foundation, as well as the building materials you select.

In cold climates, a complete foundation that extends into the ground to a depth below the frost line is usually recommended. This keeps the greenhouse from shifting or heaving during a freeze. Concrete, bricks, concrete building blocks, and stone are commonly used for this type of foundation. You may need a wooden or metal sill to fasten the greenhouse frame to; this sill would normally rest on top of the foundation. Support posts—the posts at the corners, as well as any internal posts that may be needed—can be installed directly into the foundation itself.

Some greenhouses have foundation walls that extend from ground level partway up the greenhouse wall, usually stopping at bench level. If your home has a brick or stone foundation, you may want to echo this feature in your greenhouse to help tie the two together. These partial walls are normally constructed from brick, concrete, stone, concrete building blocks, or wood; they do not need to be made of the same material as the foundation. They are especially helpful in cold climates since they insulate the lower half of the greenhouse and help keep heating costs down. Such walls do, however, eliminate any possible growing space under the benches. In mild climates, a greenhouse generally needs a foundation only as an anchor to keep the structure in position. But check with your local building department for foundation regulations; a stricter requirement may exist.

Common supports consist of 4 by 4-inch wooden posts (use larger posts if the greenhouse structure is particularly heavy—a glass and metal house, for example, weighs more than one of plastic and wood) tamped directly into the ground; wooden posts attached to concrete footings or piers; metal pipe or rods. Ingenious builders have devised various other methods —anything that effectively allows you to secure the greenhouse structure in its location is fine.

Support posts or rods should be of sufficient length to stabilize your greenhouse. If you live in a heavy wind area, posts should be long enough to be driven to a greater depth;

the kind of soil you have will also be a factor. You may want a wooden sill of 2 by 4s placed on top of the foundation or held in place by footings to attach the greenhouse frame to.

Two points to remember—wooden posts and frames are less permanent than those made from other materials, and wood must be treated with a preservative (wood treatment is discussed below).

What it's built of

Common materials for greenhouse foundations are wood, concrete, brick, concrete building blocks, stone, and metal. Any of these can form an adequate base, but check building codes for approved materials—in some areas, wood-to-ground contact is not allowed.

Wood. Redwood and cedar are the woods most commonly used in greenhouse construction, since they are naturally more resistant to rot than other woods. All types of wood, even redwood and cedar, should be treated, and copper naphthenate is the best preservative for wood being used in a greenhouse because it is not harmful to plants. Commonly available in a green color, copper naphthenate may be used as a green stain. You can apply paint over it, but you shouldn't use it over existing paint or varnish.

Wooden support posts are best stabilized with concrete footings—you can pour your own, or you can buy precast piers to be sunk into holes so the greenhouse frame rests at ground level.

Wood ranks among the more inexpensive building materials.

Concrete. Another inexpensive and easy-to-work-with material, poured concrete is a stable foundation. You will need to build forms for the structures, securing any pins, bolts, or posts in the concrete before it hardens completely.

Brick. A foundation and short wall of brick is very attractive, but depending upon your area, brick may be one of the most expensive materials you can use. It is an insulating material and will help keep heating costs down.

Concrete building blocks. Easy-to-work-with concrete building blocks are a popular foundation material ranking with the other less costly materials. Because they have air pockets, though, these blocks may permit some air or water to leak through.

Stone. Stone, like brick, creates a very attractive foundation or foundation wall. If your area has an abundance of field-stone, it can be an inexpensive material to use, but it becomes costly if the stone is not natural to your area and has to be shipped in. Stone is also a good insulator.

Metal. If metal is used in a foundation, it's most often in the form of supplemental rods or pipes. Rods attached to the greenhouse frame can simply be driven into the ground. Metal pipe can be used like a sleeve—sink pipe sections upright into the ground and fit the support post or rod into the pipe. The post or rod should fit snugly. You may want to fill in the space with gravel or poured concrete.

Rock-and-concrete retaining wall forms foundation wall of small greenhouse. Rock wall is attractive, good insulator. Gravel covers floor under plant shelves; kept wet, it helps provide humidity. Designer: Richard B. Morrall.

Wood-and-fiberglass *greenhouse (above) uses part of retaining wall as base for plant bench. Placing greenhouse on lower level permits extra height without making structure appear too large.* **Left:** *Stairstep plant bench is built directly over retaining wall. Added height in greenhouse allows for many hanging plants without obstructing gardener's head room.*

Draining away unwelcome water

Are you likely to have a problem getting rid of excess ground water around your greenhouse? If so, you should install a drainage system at the same time you put in the foundation. If you have a complete foundation, you can dig a trench around the perimeter for drain tiles or just fill the trench with gravel. In mild climates where you don't have a complete foundation, a gravel-filled trench can double as greenhouse base and drainage system.

Angle iron support post sits in concrete-filled hole. Greenhouse frame and base will be bolted to angle iron to strengthen structure. Wood-and-glass structure rests on 4 by 4-inch wood foundation.

The skeleton is important

The life expectancy of a greenhouse depends greatly on the strength and durability of its frame. The framework shapes and supports the structure and holds the wall and ceiling coverings (called "glazing") in place.

Several kinds of building materials are currently being used as greenhouse frames; the ones most commonly used are various kinds of metal and wood; recently, some plastic frames have appeared. The major differences are in cost, durability, and maintenance. How to choose? Weigh all the advantages and disadvantages presented here and choose the material with most of the qualities that count in your particular situation.

Metal is the strongest

Metal frames are generally considered to be the strongest and most substantial; they are also the most expensive. They have no capacity for retaining heat; once heated, they cool off rapidly—a problem in cold weather areas.

Metal frames are most often made of iron or aluminum. These metals vary in their acceptability as greenhouse frames.

Aluminum. A lightweight but strong metal, aluminum resists rust and other damage caused by excess moisture. Its maintenance needs are simple—give it regular cleaning and it will last for years. Aluminum is the metal most used in new greenhouses.

Iron. Iron, certainly not lightweight, is also a strong metal. And because it is subject to rust, it must be kept painted when used in a greenhouse, where constant moisture is likely to make frequent paint touchups necessary.

Prefabricated greenhouse is relatively easy for one or two people to put together (left). Wood-and-glass sections are assembled at prepared site. Corner sections are bolted together first. **Above:** *Continuous wooden strip keeps all wall panels aligned. When all walls are up, roof can be attached.*

Wood: The old favorite

Greenhouse frames made from wood are gaining popularity. Wood is a less expensive material to use than metal, and it retains absorbed heat—helpful in cooler climates. Wooden frames aren't considered as long-lasting as metal ones, but most will last a considerable time.

Redwood. Its pleasing color, as well as its natural resistance to rot, insect, and moisture damage, makes redwood frames popular for greenhouses. Redwood requires little maintenance since it needs neither paint nor stain. Many prefabricated greenhouse kits come with redwood frames.

Cedar. Cedar is also naturally resistant to rot and insect damage, but you may want to paint or stain a cedar frame for appearance. Subsequent touchups will mean more maintenance work.

Other woods. Greenhouse frames made from other types of wood are not too desirable. Like wood foundations, all wood frames will need to be treated with a preservative to make them resistant to rot and insects. Copper naphthenate is the best preservative for greenhouse use, since it isn't harmful to plants; see page 24 for further information. Even with treatment, though, the other woods may not be as long-lasting as redwood or cedar. You will probably want to paint or stain these frames.

Lath-strip panels *hold soft plastic against greenhouse frame. Panels, loosely attached with nails, are easy to remove when plastic wears out. Designer: Richard B. Morrall.*

The plastic newcomer

Greenhouse frames made from plastic, usually in the form of PVC (polyvinyl chloride) pipe, have gained favor with the do-it-yourselfer. PVC pipe is flexible, easy to work with, and relatively inexpensive. Once it's covered with rigid or soft plastic, it forms a strong, stable framework. Because of its bending property, it is frequently used in Quonset-style greenhouses; see page 9 for further information.

A plastic frame is not susceptible to rot or insect attack, and it needs neither paint nor stain. Just give it a regular cleaning to remove dirt and algae buildup.

Especially if you plan to build your own greenhouse, consider this kind of frame; its many advantages make it a promising building material.

Even-span greenhouse *has wooden frame and lower wall, fiberglass upper wall and roof. House sits on concrete block foundation. Shading material is attached to roof and walls.*

A "skin" of glass or plastic

Wall and roof coverings—coupled with the proper equipment (see pages 30-39)—are the keys to creating the greenhouse environment, since they admit natural light. What's needed is a covering of transparent or translucent material that will allow optimum light to enter. Since different plants have different light requirements, the kinds of plants you plan to grow in your greenhouse could affect your decision.

There are other considerations besides the light levels a covering permits: your climate, the cost of materials, and the durability of the material. Again, weigh carefully each possibility in relation to your particular situation.

Glass, rigid plastic, and soft plastic are the most frequently used materials for covering greenhouse walls and roofs. Occasionally, these materials are used in combination.

Glass. Glass is the standard—the covering against which all other materials are measured. It is transparent, admitting

maximum available light. (It may require shading during the summer months; see pages 38-39.) Glass is a durable covering but subject to breakage. If hail or heavy wind storms are common in your region, a glass roof could be a problem. Your framework must be square and rigid to safely support glass panes. Heaving from frost or twisting in the wind could also cause glass to break within the frame. Glass is the most expensive material you can use.

Specially treated glass is also available. Wire embedded between layers of glass forms a strong material. You can get thermal or tinted glass as well. Local building codes may require the use of these special glasses if your greenhouse is attached to your home. Treated glass is more expensive than regular glass.

Rigid plastic. Fiberglass and other types of rigid plastic—as popular as glass for covering greenhouses—are easier to cut and less subject to breakage. The light transmission through rigid plastic is good for most plants, though the light level is slightly less than it is through glass. Rigid plastic modifies the light, so no direct sunlight comes through. Recent petroleum shortages have brought increases in the cost of rigid plastic, but it's still less expensive than glass.

Rigid plastic comes in two forms: flat panels and corrugated panels. The corrugated plastic is difficult to seal. The flat panels need a good framework to prevent sagging.

Soft plastic. Polyethylene, Mylar, and other soft plastics are the least expensive greenhouse coverings. Available in a wide variety of sizes and thicknesses, they are usually purchased in rolls. Some greenhouse owners have had problems attaching the soft plastic to the frame; wherever the soft plastic is folded and wherever it's attached, it is most vulnerable to damage. Though soft plastic provides good light transmission, this may decrease with age because of yellowing or dust accumulation.

Face it—a soft plastic covering is not permanent. The life of the various soft plastics depends on their thickness, the climate, wind stress, and the craftsmanship with which the greenhouse is put together. Life expectancy of soft plastic can vary from a few months to a few years.

Soft plastic is easy to replace. Many greenhouse owners who start out with a soft plastic covering replace it with rigid plastic when it wears out.

Combination coverings. By combining some of the covering materials, you can effectively use their advantages and minimize their defects. A rigid plastic roof over soft plastic walls would produce a more durable structure than a greenhouse covered solely with soft plastic (the greenhouse roof is more vulnerable to damage than the walls). A greenhouse with glass walls and a rigid plastic roof would allow you the pleasure of a glass house with the durability of a plastic roof. In addition, rigid plastic modifies light transmission; a glass wall/rigid plastic roof combination would be especially good in hot climates where direct sunlight could damage plants. Glass and soft plastic are rarely combined.

Double walls for insulation. You can save on heating costs by using double walls in your greenhouse. A double wall between the greenhouse interior and the outdoors forms a dead air layer that serves as an insulating barrier. Some prefabricated kits come with double walls of glass or rigid plastic for this purpose. You can get the same effect by lining your own greenhouse walls with a layer of soft plastic. Some experimental greenhouses have utilized two layers of soft plastic formed into "pillows" that were inflated with air.

Whatever type of double wall insulation you use, this should be an effective method of cutting heating costs in cold climates.

Glass panes *are set into wooden frame; caulking compound holds glass in place, makes greenhouse airtight. Small nails at base of each pane prevent slipping.*

Removable wall panels *are made of soft plastic sandwiched between chicken wire on wooden frame. Lightweight, easy to handle, they provide wind protection.*

What's the floor for?

The floor of your greenhouse is both functional and aesthetic. It forms the surface you walk on, and it helps complete the image of a garden structure. Many greenhouse owners like to use such natural materials as stone or brick for the floor, since these materials seem in keeping with plants and gardening.

The walkway and the area under the benches are usually of two different materials; the walkway should form a firm, nonskid surface for walking, be easy to clean, and be durable enough to withstand constant moisture and dirt; the area under the benches is usually covered by a porous material

that can be dampened to help provide humidity. Some gardeners like to leave the soil exposed under the benches to provide additional growing space.

Common materials used for the walkway include concrete, brick, concrete building blocks, stone, gravel, wood slats, and ground bark. For under the bench areas, consider gravel, sawdust, ground bark, or any other porous material.

Some local building codes require a solid floor of concrete, but if you can possibly avoid having one, do. A solid floor supplies little humidity and eliminates any natural growing space under the benches. It's more difficult to clean, and it will boost construction costs.

Most of the flooring materials are easy to install yourself. Greenhouse suppliers and building supply stores should be able to provide instructions. An additional source of information is the *Sunset* book, How to Build Walks, Walls & Patio Floors.

Concrete. Concrete, a durable, relatively inexpensive flooring material, must be poured during the construction stage so it can set properly. It may stain badly from constant water, fertilizing, and algae formation, but it is relatively easy to clean. Some people consider it less attractive than more natural materials.

Brick. Either new or used, brick forms an attractive greenhouse floor. You can arrange it in many patterns, a few of which are pictured at bottom left. Most greenhouse owners set a brick walkway into a sand base within a wooden frame. Bricks rank among the expensive building materials, but they are easy to clean and porous enough to provide some humidity.

Concrete building blocks. Similar to a brick floor, a floor of concrete building blocks is sturdy and easy to install. The blocks are quite porous and will help provide extra humidity when dampened. Algae may grow in the air spaces, making the blocks difficult to clean. Concrete building blocks are less expensive than brick.

Stone. A walkway of stone adds to the beauty of a greenhouse; it can also add considerably to the expense if you have to buy the stones. Use stones with flat surfaces so they will be easy to walk on, and when you install them, make sure they are level and firm enough not to slip or tilt underfoot. Stones

will need cleaning to keep them free from algae and mosses. A stone walkway is pictured at bottom right.

Wooden slats. A greenhouse floor of wooden planks or slats, when wet, can be a slippery surface, risky to walk on. A wood floor, like a wood foundation or framework, needs copper naphthenate treatment to prevent moisture and insect damage. Wood is one of the less expensive materials, though, and is easy to install.

Gravel. A walkway of gravel is easy to install, functional, and like wood, economical to use. You can wet it down to provide humidity. Since it is not a solid material, you will need to rake or level it frequently to keep the walkway stable. Gravel can be difficult to clean; frequent hosings should remove dirt but could encourage the growth of moss and algae.

Gravel is a good material for use under the bench area. It holds moisture well and keeps weeds from growing. If you want to use this area for growing space later, just remove the gravel.

Ground bark. Like gravel, ground bark is inexpensive and easy to install. Because it doesn't form a solid surface, it too will need frequent maintenance to keep it level if you use it as a walkway. Unlike gravel, bark will eventually deteriorate and need replacement.

For use under the benches, ground bark is a good material. It holds moisture and will help provide some humidity. It's a good mulch and will discourage weeds.

Sawdust. Best used in the under-bench areas, sawdust is a very inexpensive, porous material that retains moisture and helps provide humidity to the greenhouse. It will eventually deteriorate. A good mulch, sawdust will keep weed growth to a minimum.

Brick walkway *in greenhouse absorbs moisture and is attractive, easy to clean. Bricks are set in bed of sand, held in place by wooden frame. Sawdust is under benches.*

Concrete path *makes firm walking surface, can be hosed off. Area under benches is covered with gravel, which is kept damp to increase humidity levels.*

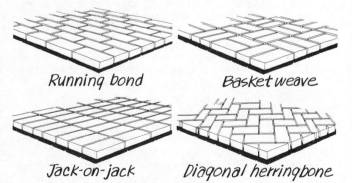

Running bond   *Basket weave*

Jack-on-jack   *Diagonal herringbone*

Four patterns *for laying bricks appear above.*

Stepping stones *give pleasant appearance, offer flat surfaces for easy walking. Stones are tamped into ground.*

A greenhouse's working parts

The amount of equipment you will need to create the proper greenhouse environment for growing plants depends on two elements: the climate outdoors and the climate you want to establish and maintain inside your greenhouse. And the climate you establish in the greenhouse will determine the kinds of plants you can grow.

Since your greenhouse will only be as effective as the climate controls you provide, it's important to get the best equipment you can afford, each item having large enough capacity to adequately handle the demands of your greenhouse.

You have no control over your area's climate, so the best advice for you to follow is the old adage, "Know your enemy." The more severe the climate you live in, the more you'll need to alter the greenhouse interior, and this means higher costs, both in the quality and capacity of the necessary equipment and in the energy required to operate it.

Your local greenhouse supplier is a good source of information on the various pieces of equipment. He knows your climate's problems, and he is familiar with the equipment you'll require to achieve the greenhouse environment you're striving for.

Most greenhouses include heating, cooling, and ventilating systems. There are few climates where these basic systems aren't needed, at least occasionally. Additional systems you may want to consider are for humidity, automatic watering and fertilizing, and artificial lighting. Select carefully the systems you want to incorporate, as they will determine the amount of control you will have over your greenhouse environment.

Warming it up

Energy is the key issue in choosing a heating system. The energy crisis is very much with us, and whichever type of heating system you select, you and your greenhouse will be at the mercy of the fuel that powers it. Fuel supplies appear to be diminishing, and the costs of purchasing those fuels continue to rise.

There are no easy answers to the energy problem at this time. Your best solution will be to select an efficient heating system that utilizes the most economical energy source available in your area. And if threatened fuel shortages become a harsh reality, a reliable emergency or auxiliary heating system will be essential.

Your options in fuel

Whichever type of heating system you choose, certain factors need to be considered: the size of your greenhouse, its location, the minimum nighttime temperature required inside the greenhouse, and your winter climate. It's also a good idea to familiarize yourself with local fuel costs; certain types of fuels are less costly in various regions, such as the relatively low cost of electricity in the Pacific Northwest.

In choosing your heating system, the first step is to contact your local greenhouse equipment supplier. Not only is he familiar with the various heating systems available, he also knows the problems you're faced with in greenhouse gardening in your area. Other good sources of information are greenhouse manufacturers' catalogues, many of which supply tables for calculating heating needs and list the BTU ratings of available heaters.

The size of heater you need will be figured by the BTU (British Thermal Unit) rating. The amount of heat needed in your greenhouse to maintain the minimum nighttime temperature during the winter months is measured in BTUs. The number of BTUs your heating system will require depends on the difference between the temperature you need inside the greenhouse and the coldest probable nighttime temperature in your area, as well as the wind factor (wind greatly increases heat loss), the size of your greenhouse (usually figured in square feet), and the heat loss factor. The building materials that make up your greenhouse determine the heat loss factor. Different materials lose heat at different rates—glass loses heat at a much higher rate than wood. Your equipment supplier or manufacturer's catalogue can usually give you the various heat loss factors for the materials in your greenhouse.

When all this data has been coordinated, you will know the number of BTUs your heating system must be capable of providing. It's a good idea to buy a slightly larger (higher number of BTUs) heating system on the chance that you may eventually want to increase the size of your greenhouse or raise the minimum nighttime temperature a few degrees. The initial extra cost of a larger heating system would be a bargain compared to installing a second system at a later date.

Next, decide which type of energy your heating system will utilize. Greenhouse heating systems in recent years have become much more sophisticated. Your most common fuel choices are between electricity and gas or oil. Solar heating is always utilized to a certain extent, but as a total system, it is still in the experimental stage. If your greenhouse is attached to your home, you may be able to extend your central heating into the greenhouse; a heating engineer can tell you if your present system is powerful enough. One innovative greenhouse gardener hooked up a wood-burning stove in a propagation greenhouse (see photograph at bottom right); this would be feasible only where wood is readily available and in milder climates where cold nights are few.

Electric heaters. Best used in small, well-built greenhouses, electric resistance heaters with fans for heat circulation are the most common electric heaters. They are controlled by a thermostat. If the thermostat is separate, locate it far enough away from the heater to give an accurate reading of the greenhouse temperature. Electric heaters can be expensive to run if your local electricity rates are high. Also, if your area is frequently hit by power outages, you will need a nonelectric alarm system and a reliable backup heating system.

Gas and oil heaters. Many greenhouse gardeners rely on gas or oil-burning heaters. These heaters should be properly vented so that no toxic fumes can harm delicate plants. Many of these heaters come with circulating fans so heat will be evenly distributed throughout the greenhouse. Again, whenever possible, locate the thermostat far enough away from the heating unit to correctly gauge the temperature. It's also a good idea to use a gas or oil system that requires no electrical connections and therefore won't be affected by a power failure.

Gas heaters utilize natural or bottled LP (liquid propane) gas. Since both natural gas and oil heaters are similar in efficiency, choose the fuel that is most economical in your area and have a reliable auxiliary system in case of fuel shortages.

Solar heat. All greenhouses receive and use some solar heat, even on cloudy days. Sunlight enters the greenhouse and heats it, but this heat eventually escapes. Greenhouses receive no solar heat at night, of course, so to keep the temperature levels up, you will need some sort of heating system.

A few experimental greenhouses are heated by solar energy alone. These require a method of storing the heat—usually by heating water kept in large tanks—so this stored heat can be used during the night. Unhappily, most of these solar-heated greenhouses are still on the drawing board (see page 36).

What if the lights go out?

Since many of the plants grown in greenhouses demand certain temperature levels, the possibility of a power outage or heating failure is downright frightening. To lessen the danger of losing plants, you should install an alarm system to warn you when the heaters fail. Equally important is being prepared to hook up an adequate back-up system.

An alarm system can indicate a faulty heater as well as warn you of a power outage. Most greenhouse alarm systems are powered by batteries, so they'll work even in a power failure. Though an alarm system isn't considered essential equipment, many greenhouse gardeners believe the margin of safety is worthwhile.

A back-up or auxiliary heating system can be a portable electric heater or kerosene-burning unit. These are easy to store and can hold back the chills until your main system can be restored.

Portable electric heater *swings into place when needed; chains between benches hold it in position.*

Roof vent *is angled metal insert that supports exhaust pipe. Opening is designed to prevent water leakage.*

Gas-powered *heating unit has fan inside to help circulate heat throughout greenhouse. Fumes are exhausted to outside.*

Wood-burning stove *helps keep temperatures from falling during those few frosty days and nights in mild climates.*

The inside story

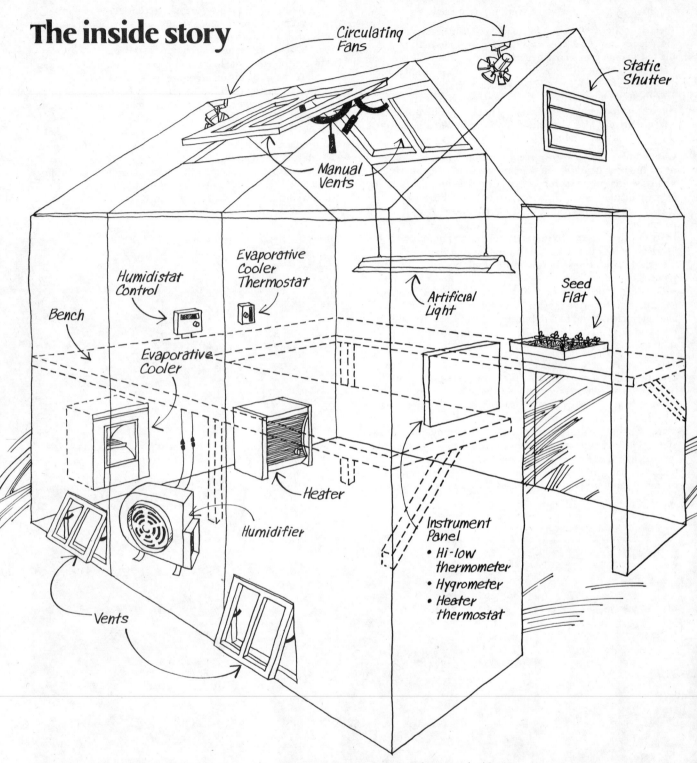

Circulating Fans

Static Shutter

Manual Vents

Evaporative Cooler Thermostat

Humidistat Control

Bench

Seed Flat

Artificial Light

Evaporative Cooler

Heater

Humidifier

Instrument Panel
• Hi-low thermometer
• Hygrometer
• Heater thermostat

Vents

Typical greenhouse equipment *is positioned to give maximum control of each system inside a 9 by 12 even-span house. Fans, vents (manually and automatically controlled) let in fresh air. Heater is centrally placed under rear bench for best heat circulation. Evaporative cooler pulls air in through wet fiber pads. Static shutter opens to let out hot air when fans operate. Humidifier disperses a moist fog, is angled for maximum coverage. Recording instruments, equipment controls are placed to give best readings.*

Environmental factors – ventilation, temperature, humidity

Keeping the greenhouse cool, especially in warm weather, and filled with fresh air is essential for good plant growth. While cooling and ventilating are separate functions within the greenhouse, the systems do overlap somewhat and are best discussed together.

Both cooling and ventilation can be accomplished by manually operated systems. You can also provide automatic systems to perform these functions. With the manual controls, the gardener will need to be constantly alert to the conditions inside his greenhouse; a greenhouse environment can quickly overheat and harm plants even on gray, overcast days. The automatically controlled systems should assure you that unexpected changes in weather will be quickly compensated for without any help from you.

Two paths to ventilation

There are two main methods of ventilating your greenhouse: one is a system of vents, the other a fan system. These systems may also be used in combination for more efficiency.

Windowlike vents are usually placed high on the greenhouse roof, at the ridge line. Secondary vents are placed near the base of the greenhouse under the benches. These vents usually come with a notched handle and a prop, or a lever with a gearwheel to open them manually. By opening these vents you set up a warm/cool air exchange and provide fresh air for the plants. Since warm air is lighter than cool air, it rises. With the top vents open, the warm air can

escape, and because the air pressure inside the greenhouse is lowered, the warm air is replaced by cool air coming in through the lower vents. This air exchange also creates air movement within the greenhouse, providing needed circulation.

Automated, this system would have the vents operated by motor-run automatic lifters triggered by a thermostat (see page 35). You would set the thermostat at the temperature level at which you wanted the vents to open. Another automatic vent opener, called a heat motor, works without electricity or wiring. It consists of a tube filled with a liquid that expands as the air temperature increases and contracts as it drops. The expanding liquid pushes a rod, and the rod opens the vent. With a dial, you set the device at the temperature level at which you want the vent to start opening.

One advantage of automatic ventilators is that they keep the greenhouse from overheating during the day; then, when the greenhouse begins to cool off in the evening, they close, trapping the remaining absorbed heat for the night.

A fan system is the second method of providing ventilation. Electric fans are placed within the greenhouse, both to remove hot, stale air and to keep the air moving.

The exhaust fan system, similar in principle to a kitchen exhaust fan, draws out the heated air. Exhaust fans are installed high, near the roof line and above plant level, to prevent drafts. A thermostat turns the exhaust fan on when a preset temperature is reached. A second vent—a jalousie window shutter—has movable horizontal flaps. When the exhaust fan starts, the flaps swing open because of air pressure

Humidifier, *sitting on bricks under bench, spreads moisture throughout 9 by 12 greenhouse.*

Artificial climate *for growing cuttings of citrus, camellias, rhodo-dendrons is achieved with gas heater, mist nozzles, fan, vent opener, humidistat; timer is at left above bench.*

differential and bring in cool air. This second vent is placed at a lower level, frequently below the benches.

The intake fan system works on the same principle, but in reverse. This system brings fresh, cool air into the greenhouse, and by changing the air pressure inside, forces the warm air out through a jalousie window shutter.

Both of these fan systems work equally well, and both require electricity to operate.

Fans for air movement are usually placed high inside the greenhouse, near the ridge line. They are angled so they won't create drafts or too much air turbulence. These fans also run on electricity.

How a greenhouse keeps its cool

The ventilation systems just described provide some cooling for the greenhouse. But in many areas, additional cooling will be needed to keep the greenhouse at the required temperature level, especially during hot weather. The cooling systems are similar in function to air conditioning used inside homes and offices, but refrigeration-type systems would be much too costly for most people to use in a greenhouse. Evaporative coolers or mist blowers are recommended methods of cooling a greenhouse.

Evaporative coolers, usually called "swamp coolers," require electricity to operate. A fan, when activated by a thermostat, pulls air into the greenhouse through wet aspen pads. This air moving through the water-soaked pads is cooled, and it absorbs some of the moisture. Not only does the evaporative cooling system cool the greenhouse, it also provides some humidity.

Mist blowers also utilize fans as part of a system that is activated by a humidistat, a device that measures moisture in the air (see page 35). The fan blows mist from a fine jet of water into the greenhouse. This mist cools the air and also provides needed humidity.

Manually operated systems can also be used, but they are dependent on the gardener's presence. You can mist your plants with a hose and a mist nozzle and wet down benches and floors to cool these surfaces; this helps cool the greenhouse by evaporation. You can install a misting system run manually or by a timer.

Shading the greenhouse will provide some cooling, too, since shading lessens the amount of sunlight and solar heat that enters the greenhouse. Unfortunately, too much shading will cause your plants to become leggy, so shading alone cannot be an adequate cooling system. Shading is discussed in more detail on pages 38-39.

Upping the moisture level

Humidity is moisture in the air, and it is a necessity since most plants grown inside the greenhouse like humidity levels around 50 to 75 percent—much higher than normal. The plants need this humidity to keep from wilting. When plants transpire, they give off moisture through their leaves. To replace this lost moisture, they need adequate moisture around their roots and adequate levels of moisture in the air. If humidity levels are low, plants will transpire more rapidly, causing them to wilt. During the day, the air inside the greenhouse warms up, and this heat reduces the humidity. To keep the moisture level high, you will have to provide humidity.

Systems for providing humidity were discussed in the preceding section on cooling the greenhouse. Both the evaporative cooling systems and the mist blowers provide humidity; the mist blower is operated by a humidistat that triggers the fan when the moisture level in the air drops. Since warm air causes lower humidity levels, the cooling systems and humidity systems overlap; both cool down the atmosphere and both provide humidity.

The manually operated systems can also be effective, but the gardener must keep a watchful eye on the hygrometer (see page 35) to make sure the humidity level doesn't drop too low and cause the plants to wilt.

Roof vent opener *opens and closes as temperatures change; control operates by thermal expansion. Hand lever hangs free, can be used manually if necessary.*

Adjustable sprinkler nozzle *is manually turned on to water potted plants, keep air humid (left).* **Right:** *Fine mist sprayer, controlled by timer, keeps cuttings moist.*

Every greenhouse needs instruments...

To help you maintain the artificial climate created inside the greenhouse, you'll need special devices to record certain parts of this environment. Since temperature and humidity levels are two of the most variable elements, you'll want instruments that record any changes in these climatic factors. Some of these instruments are used to operate the various climate systems. Other instruments you may find helpful are alarm systems and timing devices to automate various greenhouse systems.

To record temperature and relative humidity

There are two kinds of instruments used inside a greenhouse to record temperature and humidity levels: meters that record the level existent at any given time and controlling instruments used to operate various environment systems when a set temperature or humidity level is reached. Each type of instrument is important to help you keep your greenhouse functioning properly. It's a good idea to have the various systems checked periodically, to make sure they're operating at their maximum. If they are run by controlling devices (thermostats or humidistats, see below), be sure to have those instruments tested as well. Your local greenhouse equipment supplier is a good source of information.

Thermometers. A thermometer records the temperature present in the greenhouse at any given time. Since temperatures can vary within the greenhouse itself, it's a good idea to have several thermometers placed around the greenhouse at various levels. One type, a high/low thermometer, records both the highest daytime temperature and the low temperature from the night before. This type thermometer helps you analyze how effectively your systems are working. You should reset this meter daily.

To test your thermometer's accuracy, submerge the thermometer in a pail of crushed ice. At the end of 15 to 20 minutes, it should read 32° Fahrenheit or 0° centigrade. If it doesn't, discard it and buy a new one.

Thermostats. More sophisticated than thermometers, thermostats are attached to various systems that respond to heat levels, such as automatic ventilators and heaters.

When the thermostat records a preset temperature (high or low, depending on the system), the system is triggered to begin operating; it shuts off when the proper temperature level is restored. You can use your thermometers to monitor how efficiently these thermostats are working.

Hygrometers. These instruments record the relative humidity present in the air. They usually have a dial face that shows the humidity level in percents. A wet-and-dry bulb thermometer is another device used to measure relative humidity.

Humidistats. Similar to thermostats in function, these devices operate the various systems used to provide humidity. When the humidity drops below a preset level, a humidistat triggers that system to begin operating.

To trigger an alarm

If you live in a cold climate area or if your area is subject to power shortages, you may want an alarm system attached to your greenhouse heating system. If your heater fails to work for any reason, the alarm will activate. Most alarms are operated by a thermostat.

It's a good idea to get an alarm system that is battery operated. If the heater failure is due to a power outage, the alarm can still function.

To put automation to work

If you have only limited time to devote to greenhouse gardening, you'll probably want to install automatic controls to operate the many systems required. Automatic heating (pages 30-31), ventilating (pages 33-34), cooling (page 34), and humidity systems (page 34) have already been discussed. With electric timers, you can also automate systems you normally turn on by hand. These timers can operate mist sprayers, heating coils in propagating flats (see page 43), or watering systems. Automatic watering systems are effective only if the majority of your plants have the same watering needs (see pages 53-54). Otherwise, you will need to water by hand.

Humidistat electrically operates *humidifier (left); fiberglass cover protects controls from sun, moisture.* **Center:** *Wet-and-dry bulb thermometer at top and dial hygrometer at bottom measure relative humidity.* **Right:** *Timer is being set for mist sprayer (not shown). Fan at center circulates air; humidistat at right controls humidity.*

Artificial lighting–stand-in for the sun

Artificial lighting in a greenhouse can do more than merely illuminate the area. True, some gardeners install lights because they like to work in the evening or on gray, wintry days. But other greenhouse gardeners take advantage of some of the other qualities of light and use these qualities to stimulate plant growth.

To shed light on working areas, you can choose between fixtures that use incandescent bulbs and ones that use fluorescent tubes. Many greenhouse gardeners favor fluorescent fixtures (even though the initial cost of the fixtures is higher) because fluorescent light provides about three times as much light per electric watt as incandescent light. This makes fluorescent lighting more efficient and less costly.

Many greenhouse gardeners have found that artificial lighting is also effective for stimulating plant growth. You can use lights to lengthen the day (create June in January), to encourage blooming or setting of seeds or fruit, or to speed up plant growth. For these purposes, the lighting fixtures must be placed close to the plants. Because an incandescent bulb gives off heat as well as light—and excess heat could harm plants—fluorescent lights are preferred.

Whether you buy a fluorescent unit or make one, provide some method of adjusting the height to allow for plant growth and different-sized containers. Start with the tubes

Ferns, begonias, *other tender plants thrive in warm, humid, below-ground-level greenhouse. Fluorescent fixtures hanging from ceiling on each side of room provide necessary light.*

Is a solar-heated greenhouse in your future?

As our energy sources dwindle, we are accelerating our effort to find new ways to power equipment and heat buildings. Solar energy is a promising substitute that seems almost certain to be used increasingly in the future. Described, most simply, as the sun's rays heating the earth's surface, it involves the process of trapping the sun's energy, storing it, and using it when it's needed—at night and on cloudy days, for example.

Once a system has been set up, solar heating is an economical form of power that makes use of a free energy source, the sun. Ideas for two possible systems are outlined below.

The first method entails locating heat collecting panels, which contain water, on the roof of a home. Usually panels sit on top of the building they heat, but the structure of most greenhouses couldn't support their weight. Also, the panels would prevent quite a bit of sunlight from entering the greenhouse—sunlight that is necessary for normal plant growth and at least part of the heating.

The collector panels, usually painted black for maximum absorbing power, trap radiant heat and transmit it to water in tubes. During the day, pumps slowly circulate water from a storage tank, through the tubes, and back to the tank, where the energy is stored as hot water.

The house and greenhouse could share a common energy storage tank that would supply solar heat to both structures.

In the greenhouse, pumps circulate hot water through thin-walled tubes located just under the benches. Heat given off by the water in the tubes warms the greenhouse. During warm weather months, you'd have to run the pumps only at night. In cold climates you would need an auxiliary heating system to keep temperature levels up.

The other idea for trapping the sun's energy is much simpler. It uses a wall made of rock, brick, or some other absorbent material within your greenhouse to absorb solar heat. A lean-to is the best greenhouse shape for this purpose; in this case it would "lean" against the heat storage wall.

Build the absorbing wall the height of your greenhouse with the broad side facing south, if possible. Paint the wall black for maximum heat absorption. During the day the wall absorbs solar radiation as the sunlight comes in through the greenhouse roof and walls. At night the wall radiates its absorbed heat and keeps the greenhouse warm. Putting an insulation cover over the greenhouse on cold nights is very helpful; otherwise the glass will conduct some of the stored heat from the greenhouse back to the atmosphere.

In both cases—as with any greenhouse—a ventilating system will be necessary to remove excess heat accumulated during hot days (see pages 33-34). The stored energy from the collecting-panel system could be used to run the cooling devices and open vents. In this way you make use of the energy when a maximum amount is available— during the warm summer months.

Always have an extra heater (electric or gas) available for emergencies; something could go wrong with your solar system or the weather might be heavily overcast for several days.

Solar heat is a promising energy source. Relatively few systems are on the market now, but the future should bring many new developments. Keep your eye out for solar heating systems—and think about how you could adapt one to your greenhouse.

Double-decker benches, *constructed of 2 by 4s and scrap lumber, hold large collection of African violets. Aluminum foil reflects light from fluorescent fixtures onto plants. Designer: Emory Leland.*

6 to 12 inches above the plant foliage. If the foliage starts to bunch together unnaturally, plants are receiving too much light. If they become leggy, they need more light. Since fluorescent light will not harm plants, the unit may be set as close as needed.

Ordinary fluorescent lights can supply sufficient light for plant growth. You can also buy special fluorescent tubes that have been developed to simulate actual sunlight rays; these special tubes are used to stimulate plants to bloom, produce fruit, and set seeds. Such tubes are more expensive than regular fluorescent tubes; you'll find them in most garden centers or hardware stores.

Fluorescent lighting fixtures need a white or foil reflector to direct light onto plants. When placing plants or flats under light, remember that the light is strongest at the center of the tube. Several fluorescent tubes placed side by side are best; one tube alone will have little, if any, effect.

Occasionally, incandescent light bulbs are used to heat a propagating box or keep the temperature above freezing in an unheated coldframe or very small greenhouse. Only incandescent lights will serve for this purpose, as fluorescent lights give off very little heat.

Fluorescent lights *above assortment of potted vegetables keep third grade's class project a happy success during cold winter months. Fixtures were raised as plants grew.*

Basement corner *is used to grow chives, leaf lettuce, oregano, parsley, peppers, and tomatoes from seed. Fluorescent fixtures hanging from chains provide necessary light.*

The many ways to shade a greenhouse

Why shade your greenhouse? The reasons are twofold: to protect plants from the direct rays of the hot summer sun and to help keep the greenhouse cool (see page 34). There are numerous ways of providing the needed shade, all equally satisfactory. Some will require more maintenance than others.

Whitewashing the greenhouse is perhaps the most widely used method of providing shade. Sometime in mid or late spring, a white paintlike solution is brushed or sprayed on the exterior of the glass parts of the greenhouse (coverings of rigid or soft plastic usually aren't whitewashed). The solution can be a commercial whitewash made for use on greenhouses or a white, cold-water paint. Apply the whitewash like paint. One greenhouse gardener used his tank-type sprayer to apply it (see photograph on facing page). Be sure you completely clean out the sprayer, both before and after using it for this purpose. Whatever type whitewash you use, it will gradually wear off, thanks to rain and watering chores. If it hasn't all washed off by midautumn, scrape off any remaining paint; your plants will need all the winter light they can get.

Because both rigid and soft plastic coverings modify the light before it enters the greenhouse, they usually require less shading than glass. All the following methods of shading work equally well on all types of greenhouses.

Blinds made of wooden strips, bamboo, or aluminum slats provide good shade on hot, sunny days. Since these can be rolled up and down whenever you wish, you can open up or shade the greenhouse at any time. Most of these shade blinds are operated manually.

Panels made of lath strips can be attached to the greenhouse during the summer. These panels provide adequate shade and can be put up or taken down whenever you wish. Storage could be a problem if the panels are large.

Shade cloth or saran cloth is available from greenhouse equipment suppliers. Made from green or black plastic, shade cloth can be used in numerous ways. It comes in a variety of meshes, each providing a certain percentage of shade, from light to heavy. You can stretch shade cloth on a wooden frame and suspend it over the greenhouse, cut shade cloth panels the size of the plastic or glass panes and tack the shade cloth to the frame, or stretch the cloth directly above the plants. You can also affix it to the glass or rigid plastic by wetting the glass and applying the shade cloth to the glass with a squeegee. When you need to remove it, you just pull the shade cloth off.

There is also an aluminum blind-type shade cloth you can attach to the greenhouse frame or a separate framework. It provides good shade but is more expensive than the plastic shade cloth.

Depending on your climate, you may want to shade only some of the plants in your greenhouse. The best method of partial shading is to stretch pieces of shade cloth only over the plants that require shade, such as ferns. One gardener places lath strips on a metal framework inside her greenhouse to shade lettuce and other tender vegetables; tomatoes and other sun-loving plants are left uncovered.

Several types of greenhouse shading are pictured below and on the next page. Study each of these methods to find the one that best suits your needs.

Whitewash applied *to glass surfaces, protects plants from summer heat. Extended handle attached to paint roller makes it easy for gardener to reach highest spots of greenhouse.*

Lath strips *shade front and left side of roof—both exposed to year-round bright sunlight. Lean-to on right side protects cymbidium collection from winter frosts.*

Shade cloth *is attached to roof support beams, protects shade-loving ferns, begonias from sunburn. Greenhouse sides are enclosed with corrugated plastic.*

Whitewash is sprayed *onto glass roof panels. Gardener uses tank-type sprayer. Tank should be thoroughly cleaned before and after use.*

Redwood frame *supports covering of shade cloth 2 feet above glass-paneled roof; space between roof and shading allows vents to open and close.*

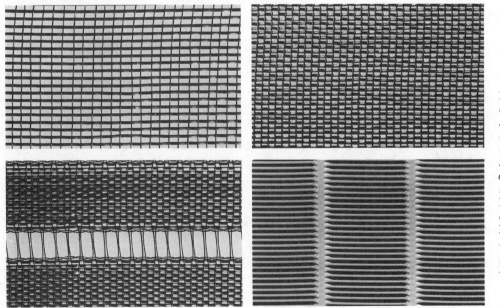

Plastic or aluminum *shade cloth creates light-to-heavy shade, depending on its density. Plastic shade cloth (top left) gives 47 percent shading.* **Top right:** *Denser cloth creates 73 percent shade, is popular in warm climates.* **Lower left:** *Patterned plastic shade cloth gives 73 percent shade.* **Lower right:** *Aluminum shade cloth—more expensive than plastic cloth—creates heavy shade, is long lasting.*

Furnishing your greenhouse

With the greenhouse structure completed and the climate control equipment installed, you can turn to planning the greenhouse interior. The two most important items are plant benches and storage areas. Properly planned storage and sturdy, well-placed benches can make your greenhouse gardening much more enjoyable.

Benches for display

Greenhouse benches are tablelike structures placed around the interior perimeter of the house at about counter height. They are used to hold plants, propagating trays, and seed flats. If there is room, another bench can be placed in the center of the greenhouse (aisles should be from 2 to 3 feet wide for easy maneuvering).

Bench tops are usually constructed with regularly spaced openings that allow air to circulate freely around the plants and their containers. Benches are frequently made of wooden slats or lath, either redwood or cedar. If other woods are used, they must be treated with a preservative to prevent damage from moisture and insects (see page 24 for information on wood preservatives). Some benches have wooden frames with wire or hardware cloth coverings. Occasionally bench frames or legs are made of metal. Several bench styles are shown below and on the next page.

Greenhouse benches are usually attached to the walls of the greenhouse and are between 2 and 3 feet deep. You need to be able to reach to any part of your benches easily; if benches aren't included in the greenhouse kit, design yours to be a good height and depth for you.

Some benches are built like stairsteps; each "step" is a 1 by 4-inch or 1 by 6-inch board—wide enough to hold one row of plants. The next "step" up (usually about 8 inches higher) holds another row of plants. This is an efficient way to save space, since you can get many more plants on the vertical stairsteps than you could on a flat bench using the same amount of floor space. An example of the stairstep bench is pictured at right.

Your greenhouse benches will have to be strong enough to hold all the plants you plan to grow. Use adequate support posts to hold the benches securely, and check them periodically for signs of decay or structural weaknesses.

If you use the space under the benches for growing plants, you will need to protect those plants from excess water dripping from the bench above. Here's a good way to do it: attach a drip tray made of fiberglass or metal to the underside of the bench, angled so the water runs to the back of the bench, channeling excess water away. This trap will still allow for good air circulation through the bench openings.

Stairstep benches *increase plant space, make plants easy to reach, water. Each bench holds one row of plants; bench rails are 1 by 4s.*

Easy-to-make benches *illustrated below have regularly spaced openings, allowing air to circulate under and around plants.*

Lath frame on sawhorses

Hardware cloth bench top

Slat-top bench

Aluminum wire rests on bench tray of corrugated fiberglass and holds pots, flats of potted seedlings. Tray, angled so water drains off, is supported by 1 by 4 frame.

Lower-than-usual custom-built benches suit height of owner, ease the reach to pots on space-stretching step-up rear shelves.

What gardener doesn't need storage?

Greenhouse gardening, like other types of gardening, requires special tools, plant containers, potting mixes, fertilizers, and so forth. You can have all this equipment handy when you need it if you provide adequate storage space either within the greenhouse itself or in an adjacent or nearby area.

Some gardeners find the handiest spot is inside the greenhouse, either under the benches or on an unused bench or wall. If your greenhouse has solid walls up to the bench level, under-bench storage is perfect, and it won't look messy from the outside.

The various ingredients for potting mixes should be kept dry; covered plastic garbage cans work well for this type of storage. Garden tools and other small items can hang from hooks on a pegboard. Keep pesticides, fertilizers, and other chemicals tightly sealed and in a closed cabinet for safety. Be sure these chemicals are clearly labeled. Hoses and other watering equipment should be rolled up or stored out of the pathway when not in use.

Many gardeners combine a storage area with a potting bench for needed work space. Three greenhouse work areas are pictured at right and below.

Cement laundry sink, fitted into sturdy custom-built bench, is handy for cleaning and disinfecting plant containers. Plumbing is connected to sprinkler pipes just outside greenhouse wall. Child's wagon is perfect for transporting heavy loads.

Shallow cabinet in garden room hides plumbing for water faucets, also provides storage for garden tools, fertilizers, other garden chemicals.

Garden work center inside greenhouse has salvaged sink-drainboard combination for potting, other chores. Tools hang from nails on wall above, rest against slat cross brace.

Other structures for growing plants

Greenhouses aren't the only garden structures used for growing plants. Coldframes, shade or lath houses, and garden rooms can also alter your climate, creating an artificial atmosphere that promotes plant growth.

Coldframes—and their heated versions, hotbeds—are very useful for starting seeds and cuttings and protecting them from cold or frosty weather.

Shade or lath houses modify sunlight, providing the proper light for growing shade-loving plants. You can cover a shade house with soft plastic during the winter and gain some cold weather protection.

A garden room is an extension of your house designed for both plants and people. This room has increased light levels and controlled temperature levels to accommodate growing plants indoors.

Some like it cold – some like it hot

Experienced gardeners consider a coldframe an indispensable tool for successful year-round gardening. In fact to many, a well-built, well-tended coldframe is nearly as useful as a small greenhouse. And it takes up far less space and will cost almost nothing if you build it with scrap lumber.

A coldframe can be anything from a simple frame with a cover of plastic sheeting to a more elaborate structure with its own heat source. You may want to start with a fairly simple frame until you see just how much you'll use it.

If you are handy with tools you might consider building the large coldframe shown at the bottom of the page. It will

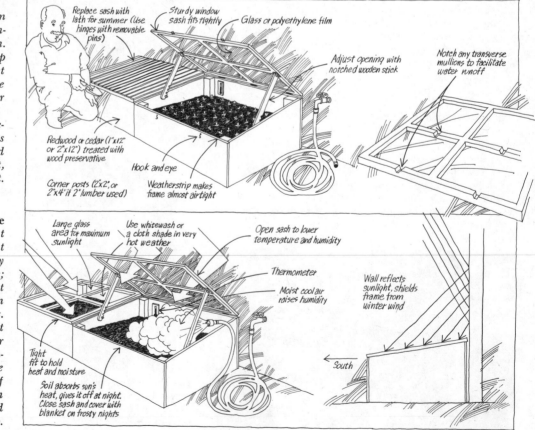

Large coldframe *can substitute for greenhouse in small garden. In hot weather, prop glass cover open to let excess heat escape (thermometer at rear should stay about 80°).*

Lath cover or whitewash on glass also keeps heat down. In cold weather or at night, close cover to trap heat.

Replace sash with lath for summer (Use hinges with removable pins)

Sturdy window sash fits tightly

Glass or polyethylene film

Adjust opening with notched wooden stick

Notch any transverse mullions to facilitate water runoff

Redwood or cedar (1"x12" or 2"x12") treated with wood preservative

Hook and eye

Corner posts (2"x2", or 2"x4" if 2" lumber used)

Weatherstrip makes frame almost airtight

Cover of coldframe *keeps heat in. Light rays (white arrows) at left pass directly through glass panels; rays indicated at right bounce off wall, then pass through glass. With top shut, heat increases. To lower temperatures in summer, use mist nozzle and very light flow of water. To retain trapped heat on cold nights, cover glass top.*

Large glass area for maximum sunlight

Use whitewash or a cloth shade in very hot weather

Open sash to lower temperature and humidity

Thermometer

Moist cool air raises humidity

Wall reflects sunlight, shields frame from winter wind

Tight fit to hold heat and moisture

Soil absorbs sun's heat, gives it off at night. Close sash and cover with blanket on frosty nights

South

take you a day to put it together—maybe even less time if you have some old windows or a glass door on hand.

Hotbed is made with wooden flat (above), inverted bottoms of coffee cans placed over wired-together light bulbs; slotted sides of cans fit neatly over wires. Make sure wires are insulated and sockets remain dry. Place flat of cuttings on top of hotbed.

A coldframe works in any climate

In milder climates, coldframes protect plants against frost and help keep temperatures warm enough for proper plant growth through the winter. In cold winter areas, they will give the same results provided the unit has an auxiliary heating system. If so, the structure is commonly known as a hotbed. The text on these two pages uses the term coldframe exclusively; however, if you live in a cold climate, the term also means hotbed.

Whatever your climate, a coldframe is especially useful for early planting of summer annuals and seeds, protecting tender plants in winter, forcing cuttings to root faster, starting perennials from seed in summer, and growing many kinds of plants you wouldn't otherwise attempt to grow.

How can a structure consisting of four walls and a transparent roof make all this possible? The answer is simple: that a coldframe acts as a controlled weather capsule in which temperature, humidity, and light are kept within the limits favorable for plant growth. In addition, it protects tender seedlings and cuttings from attacks by pests and birds and from damage by wind or hail.

What a coldframe does

A coldframe traps heat by admitting sunlight during the day through its transparent or translucent covering of glass or plastic and by retaining heat radiated from the surrounding soil during the cold night hours. Also, the nearly airtight structure keeps loss of moisture through evaporation to a minimum, cutting down on your watering chores. The simplest piece of garden equipment that employs this principle of a heat and moisture trap is the hotcap, a dome of heavy wax paper used to protect tomatoes, melons, and other young plants from the possibility of late spring frosts. Other simple methods of providing frost protection are discussed on pages 48-49.

Start with a plan

In planning a coldframe, start with the dimensions of the cover. If you are not restricted to a certain size, choose

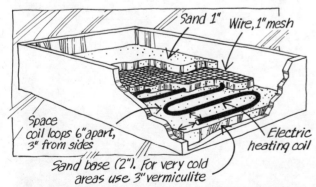

Labels: Sand 1", Wire, 1" mesh, Space coil loops 6" apart, 3" from sides, Electric heating coil, Sand base (2"). For very cold areas use 3" vermiculite

Propagating tray *has electric heating cable placed on sand base, covered with mesh wire and sand layer.*

dimensions that will fit some multiple of a standard planting flat. Flats come in several sizes, but two commonly used types measure 14½ by 23½ inches and 18½ by 18½ inches. Make your frame with enough leeway so you can lift flats in and out without pinching your fingers.

If you want to use scrap pieces of lumber and glass you have on hand, then the size of your coldframe will be dictated by the dimensions of these pieces. (You can also buy ready-made window sash, usually 3 by 6 feet, or snap-together aluminum sash in which you install polyethylene plastic.)

The walls can be made of scrap lumber, or you can buy the cheapest grade of new lumber. Redwood and cedar are long lasting and rot and insect resistant; other types of wood can also be used if you treat them with a preservative (see page 24). Either 1 by 12 or 2 by 12 lumber is practical. Fit the corners as tightly as you can; or, to make sure no heat escapes, caulk the edges with asphalt emulsion.

Where should it go?

Because the coldframe is heated by the sun, you must slope the cover toward the south. If you can, build the structure so there is a wall or fence on the north side; you'll protect the frame from winds and cut down on loss of heat. To increase the light level within the frame, paint the fence or wall a light color or paint the coldframe interior sidewalls white or silver.

Whatever location you choose for your coldframe, make sure it's not in a part of the garden that has poor drainage, since you don't want water to collect in or around the frame after rains.

Other equipment you'll need

A good thermometer is essential if you want your coldframe to work. Most plants that will grow well outdoors in North America will continue growing at temperatures from about 40° to 100° and do best at about 85°. When your thermometer reaches 85°, you can prop open the top of the frame to let out some heat. Then in late afternoon, when the outside temperature starts to fall, shut the top to trap the heat radiated by the soil. In really hot weather you'll have to whitewash the glass or make a second cover of lath to cut down on the light.

The possible dream – a shade house

Similar to a greenhouse, the shade or lath house alters the climate to accommodate growing plants. It doesn't have complete climate control, but it does offer shade and wind protection. Occasionally a gardener will cover a shade house with soft plastic in the winter to provide some frost protection. Even with its limited control, a shade house can be a very useful garden structure.

Usually constructed of lath strips nailed to a framework at regularly spaced intervals, a shade house is a two or three-sided shelter used to protect delicate plants from sun and wind. Depending on your particular summer climate, many plants can be successfully grown in this type of structure. Fuchsias, tuberous begonias, ferns, and any other plants that require shade instead of full sun are candidates.

If wind isn't a problem, a patio roof made of lath strips or some other covering will provide needed shade. But for the most part, a three-sided structure is the most functional. Some gardeners attach the shade house to a fence, using the fence as one of the shelter's walls; this cuts down somewhat on construction costs. You can also attach benches to the walls and hang plants from the walls and ceiling to make a shade house more versatile.

If you live in a mild climate area, you can utilize a shade house the year around. If your climate is harsh, the shade house will be a welcome retreat on hot summer days. If you leave enough room in it for some lawn furniture, your shade house can do double duty as a sheltered patio.

Some gardeners use their shade houses as makeshift greenhouses or large coldframes during the winter months. By covering the structure with soft plastic, you can provide some frost protection. The plastic will have to be firmly anchored so that wind or rain won't damage it. Other gardeners use the shade house as a winter shelter for tender plants in containers.

It's a good idea to have a water faucet in or near your shade house to simplify watering. This plumbing extension should be installed at the same time the shade house is built. You may also want an electrical hookup in the shade house so you can have lights or a portable heater.

Lean-to lath house *filters sunlight for large collection of fuchsias. Lath strips are nailed to frame of 2 by 4s. Floor is poured concrete. Gates at either end allow easy access.*

Slanted roof *of lath strips supported by 2 by 4 frame shades bed of begonias (both tuberous and fibrous), hanging fuchsias. Rear wall is fence covered with peg board.*

Access *to plants in lath-covered structure is achieved by removal of four 1 by 10 boards held in place at top and bottom by angled 1 by 2 blocks. Watering of plants is controlled automatically.*

Lath strips *attached to curved inset on 4 by 4 support posts filter the light—a must for growing staghorn ferns outdoors. Ferns hang on solid grapestake fence.*

Lath cover *of 2 by 2s (left) protects plants from summer heat.* **Right:** *Shelter folds up, hooks to fence when not needed.*

Shade house *protects fuchsias from sunburn. One side is house wall; other walls, roof are made of lath strips attached to 1 by 4 frame.*

Patio between two greenhouses *has lath-covered peaked roof to protect shade-loving plants. Center roof support is ideal place for hanging baskets.*

The garden room: where plants cozy up to people

A garden room is designed for plants as well as people. And since it's part of your house, the garden room must do more than just house plants: it must also provide living space. Many garden rooms do double duty as breakfast rooms, dining rooms, entertaining areas, family rooms, and sitting rooms; some ingenious indoor gardeners incorporate the garden room into their bathrooms.

If the garden room is to be a new addition to your house, be sure to get a building permit. Under local codes the ratio of glass to solid building materials may be limited, or you may be required to install thermal-pane glass or wire-reinforced glass.

Make the environment work two ways

Because people share the living space with plants in a garden room, you won't want to provide the perfect tropical environment. Warm temperatures coupled with high humidity would suit your indoor plants perfectly, but most people would find this atmosphere unpleasant, if not intolerable. Luckily, you and your plants can strike a bargain.

Light is the key factor for growing plants successfully. In the average American house or apartment, most rooms provide inadequate light. The best the indoor gardener can do is to group plants around the best-lit windows or install artificial lighting to help the situation. But because the garden room is designed with the growing of plants as one of its main objectives, providing adequate light will be a major consideration. Abundant window area and possibly a glass ceiling or skylights will bring in more than ample light for tropical foliage plants. In fact, you may even need to provide some shade on hot summer days (see pages 38-39)

Heating should be no problem. Most people extend their regular house heating system into the garden room. Tropical foliage plants grown indoors usually like the same temperatures as people. Temperature levels between 70° and 75° during the day and around 65° at night should please all the occupants.

Most plants need good ventilation—that means doors and windows that can be opened to let stuffy hot air escape. You may also want to install a circulating fan. Fortunately, most garden rooms are of sufficient size to avoid too much trapped hot air, making large-scale ventilation unnecessary.

Though you don't want a sticky, moist atmosphere in your garden room, your plants will want some humidity. Most tropical plants grown indoors can get by with levels around 30 to 40 percent, and you can provide this humidity level without sophisticated equipment. A number of plants grouped together will help provide humidity to each other through transpiration—plants give off moisture through

Long and narrow, *this window-walled garden room was once entrance to house (above). Room holds collection of tropical plants, vegetables; doubles as breakfast and sitting room.* **Left:** *Beamed ceiling has glass panes reinforced with wire mesh. Plastic laminate floor is easy to clean and moisture resistant. Though solar heat usually is sufficient, vents from house's central heating system can be opened for added warmth.*

their leaves as a natural process. Misting your plants will also help. And humidity trays—watertight trays made of plastic or metal, holding pebbles or rocks that are kept constantly moist—are still another way to keep humidity levels up.

How do you choose wall and floor building materials and furniture for a garden room? You start by remembering that water and dirt will be everywhere. Materials should be impervious to moisture damage and should be easy to clean. One devoted indoor gardener designed a garden room with aggregate flooring that could just be hosed down (see photograph on page 88); the owner even provided a drain.

If you have a great number of plants, a storage and potting area with a water faucet would be extremely useful. For plant containers, potting mix, fertilizers, and the other garden paraphernalia most plant lovers collect, plan storage that will keep everything close at hand. And a water faucet with a hose will make your watering chores much more manageable.

Plants that take to a garden room

Because the climate can't be controlled as specifically as a greenhouse environment, the plants you grow in a garden room must be adapted to less-than-perfect conditions. Many of the plants commonly grown in garden rooms are those grown as "tropicals" or house plants. These are plants native to tropical or semitropical areas, able to grow in lower light levels and adjust to a less-than-perfect environment. They are usually grown for their foliage rather than their flowers or fruit.

A listing of the most common plants included in a garden room can be found on pages 89-91; but any plant you grow indoors, even the hardiest, will probably prefer the environment your garden room provides.

Sliding glass doors of garden room open onto brick patio **far left.** *During warm summer months, bamboo screen over half of glass roof panels shades collection of tropical plants.* **Left:** *Narrow shelves hold plants next to louvered window that provides air circulation.*

Glass roof, window wall *provide ample light for artist's work and for large plant collection. Plants sit on floor or on low wooden benches. Tiled floor is easy to clean after watering chores.*

Tropical plants in bathroom *enjoy light from ceiling fixtures, humidity produced from daily shower use. Watering is done with garden hose stored next to cabinet.*

How to give Jack Frost the run-around

The cold nights and clammy soil of early spring often keep melons, peppers, squash, and tomatoes, as well as annuals and other summer plants, from growing much, even if daytime air is warm. When it's icy cold, hardier plants like peas and lettuce will grow slowly, too.

You can give these seedlings a head start and plant up to a month earlier if you effectively shield them from the cold. Plant protectors—actually miniature greenhouses—work on the same principle as a regular greenhouse, trapping heat and light and setting up an artificial environment. The extra warmth around plants helps establish them and keeps them growing faster, so they'll mature 2 to 3 weeks earlier. In addition to early spring use, these instant greenhouses can be employed in the fall to extend the producing season of vegetables, especially tomatoes and, when it gets really cold, lettuce.

Wax paper tents are available commercially, but for effectiveness and longevity they can't compare to these homemade protectors. And when you make them yourself, types of plant protectors are limited only by your imagination. Five easy-to-make protectors are described below.

Dome umbrellas. These good-looking protectors have the advantage of folding up for easy storage; they were originally clear plastic dome umbrellas. Between uses, let them dry completely and then dust them with unscented talcum powder before storing.

You can buy umbrellas with handles that slip off and on; that way they can always be reconverted for conventional use. If your umbrellas have firmly attached handles, you can use wire cutters to snip through the handle just above the curve; then glue the U-shaped handle onto the top of the dome (see photograph at right). The center pole is still long enough to stick into the ground several inches.

At night and during cold weather, push the umbrella down until the plastic dome firmly touches soil on all sides. On warm days, pull the umbrella up several inches to let air circulate inside—otherwise, plants may cook.

Glass jugs. These one-plant greenhouses are clear gallon jugs with their bottoms removed. Clear glass is better than tinted glass, because it permits more light to enter.

If you don't have a bottle-cutting kit, try this method to remove the bottom: soak a piece of coarse twine in kerosene, tie it around the bottom of the jug, and set it on fire. As soon as it burns out, plunge the jug into cold water. The bottom should drop off. Since the rough edges will be buried in soil, they shouldn't pose a threat to unwary children or pets.

Remove bottle caps to allow air and heat to circulate; replace them when you expect weather to get cold enough to damage plants.

Gallon glass jugs with bottoms cut off protect lettuce seedlings when weather is still cold and frosty. Jugs must be removed during the day so tender plants won't burn.

Transparent dome-shaped umbrellas *protect tender seedlings from cold spring nights, unexpected late frosts; are removed daily for ventilation.*

Minihothouse. Effective for any plants, this structure is especially useful if you grow tomatoes. It can be used over seedlings to give them an early start and over mature plants to prolong fruiting in the fall.

The hothouse is easy to use—just put it over the plants on cool nights and take it off on warm days. By trapping heat normally lost at night, it keeps plants warmer than if they were left exposed to open air. This also permits blossoms to set and bear fruit even when the nighttime temperature drops below 55°.

To make a hothouse similar to the one shown at right, make a frame of rough redwood 1 by 2s and cover it with clear plastic film. A hothouse that measures 2 by 2 by 4 feet should be big enough for a single plant. You might want to make a larger frame to protect several plants at once.

Lath frame. The merits of this easy-to-build structure are twofold: plants can be protected from the cold, and vines will be supported later on—fruit won't lie in the mud and rot.

Make a frame like the one pictured, using lumber scraps—broken bean poles, broomsticks, or lath strips will do. Cover the frame with a plastic drop cloth or an old bed sheet. Tie the corners of the cover to the frame legs so it won't blow off in a wind. When the weather warms, remove the frame. For cucumbers or squash you can leave the frame (minus the covering) to support the plants during the summer; the vines will spread over the top of the framework.

Strawberry protector. The hinged roof pictured here is a must if you live in a frosty winter area and want to harvest a midwinter strawberry crop.

The purpose of the roof is to shield the plants from frosty nights. Because it lets light and heat through in the daytime, a clear plastic covering serves well. And a hinge keeps the roof attached and allows it to slope so rain water can run off.

For this shelter, clear polyethylene film, at least 4 mils thick, is encased within a double frame of lath strips or 1 by 2s. Nail or screw a 2 by 2-inch strip to the wall behind the strawberry box, about 4 feet above the ground. Attach the frame to the 2 by 2 with at least two hinges, more if the roof length requires additional support. Finally, attach a piece of small-link chain to the outer edge of the frame and to the building, 6 to 8 inches above the 2 by 2 (see photo) to hold the cover in place

Minihothouse has frame of 1 by 2s, flat fiberglass sides, top; protects tomato plant in raised bed from frost, prolongs harvest. Corrugated metal strip in soil keeps covering in place.

Lath frame *has corrugated fiberglass on top, translucent soft plastic on three sides. Open end faces downwind; cover it if hard frost is likely.*

Strawberry protector *of translucent soft plastic sandwiched between double frame of 1 by 2s protects container of strawberries from frost, helps extend plants' normal growing season.*

GARDENING IN THE GREENHOUSE

Once you've gardened in a greenhouse, you'll be amazed you ever managed without one. Your plants will thrive, produce flowers, and even bear fruit as never before. And you can garden the year around, unhampered by the weather.

This second section looks at the many kinds of gardening you can accomplish inside a greenhouse environment. You can, of course, grow exotic plants with beautiful foliage and exquisite flowers. But your greenhouse gardening can also take on more practical functions. You can start summer annuals and vegetables from seed in the early spring (or fall) and have well-established seedlings to plant outdoors when the weather warms up. You can increase your plant collections by propagating new plants from cuttings. You can even use part of your greenhouse to grow some vegetables to maturity.

One aspect of greenhouse gardening that appeals to many people is the ability to grow tropical plants that wouldn't survive without the controlled environment. With a greenhouse, you can create the proper climate for these specialized plants.

The greenhouse gardener is truly fortunate. Once he has mastered the art of greenhouse gardening, he can grow just about any plant he chooses at any time, thanks to the fact that he can create the proper environment and control it.

Backyard greenhouse *contains tropical foliage plants, orchids, cuttings, and seedlings. Greenhouse has wooden frame covered with translucent fiberglass. Slatted benches provide drainage.*

Techniques of greenhouse gardening

Gardeners everywhere are at the mercy of the climates in which they live: they depend on their weather for their heat and sunlight; they are bound by the seasons as to the flowers and vegetables they can grow; and when the snows and frost come, they are confined to a few hardy standbys and some house plants.

But there is one type of gardener who has none of these limitations: the greenhouse gardener. He or she gardens in a controlled environment where temperature levels are constant, humidity and ventilation are provided, and with artificial lighting, even day length can be controlled.

The following section discusses the hows of gardening in a controlled environment. Some of it sounds much like other types of gardening, since potting mixes, plant containers, and fertilizers are used in the greenhouse, too. But this basic gardening information is tailored specifically to help the greenhouse gardener gain quick mastery of the art of gardening in a controlled environment.

Soils are basic

Most greenhouse gardeners grow their plants in containers, which can be moved around easily and dealt with on an individual basis. This kind of gardening requires large amounts of lightweight potting soil.

Commercially packaged potting mixes are sold at nurseries and garden centers in packages of varying sizes, the larger bags being the most economical.

Many greenhouse gardeners find it more convenient to make up their own potting mixes. This way they can handle their plants' needs on an individual basis by altering their basic mix slightly.

A good potting soil should contain ample nutrients for healthy plant growth; it should be easy for roots to penetrate and it should drain well, yet retain sufficient moisture to keep the plant from wilting. A popular basic mix consists of 2 parts good garden soil, 1 part sharp river sand, and 1 part peat moss or other form of organic matter. Some gardeners add bone meal or complete fertilizers. To grow plants that prefer an acid soil, such as azaleas or camellias, use a mix that contains at least 50 percent organic matter (peat moss, leaf mold, or finely ground bark). Never use a clay soil in a container mix.

Many greenhouse gardeners prefer to use a uniform, predictable potting mix that contains no garden soil. Because garden soil can carry diseases, insect eggs, or larvae, it needs to be sterilized by baking before you can use it, and this can be both time-consuming and messy.

A good artificial soil mix for the greenhouse is the U.C. Mix. The basis for this mix is a combination of fine sand, perlite, or vermiculite mixed with peat moss, sawdust, or ground bark. Fertilizer is added. This mix gives excellent aeration (provides air around the plant roots) and drainage, and it holds moisture well. The various ingredients are free of soil-borne diseases and insects.

Because this mix leaches quickly, you will need to fertilize your plants regularly and water carefully. If you would like to use the U.C. Mix, write to Agricultural Cooperative Extension, Public Service, University of California, 1422 South 10th, Richmond, CA 94804. Ask for Manual 23; there may be a small fee.

Clay pots, plastic pots

Most greenhouse gardeners use either clay or plastic containers in the greenhouse. Both are relatively inexpensive and will do the job. They do have some differences, and you should understand how each container works before making your choice.

Here are some general points to keep in mind: 1) Plant containers for the greenhouse need a drainage hole in the bottom of the pot; 2) Some plants grow better in one type pot than another—be aware of your plant's special needs; 3) Plant containers will need to be cleaned and sterilized between uses; do this by scrubbing the insides with a mixture of bleach and water, and leave the containers in the sun for several days to kill any fungus spores that may lurk in tiny openings.

If slugs, snails, or earthworms are a real problem in your greenhouse, place a small piece of very fine mesh wire screening over the container drainage holes. This should keep any creatures from crawling in through the pot bottom. It will also help drainage.

Clay pots. That old standby, the red clay pot, continues to be a popular container. It's easy to find and comes in many shapes and sizes.

Clay pots are porous, allowing them to absorb moisture and permit air circulation through the container sides. It's difficult to overwater plants in clay pots. If plants are overfertilized, though, excess salts will appear as a white crust on the pot sides. In areas where the water has a heavy salt concentration, the excess salts filter out, also forming a white crust on the container sides. In humid greenhouses, a green moss or mold may also form. These crusts should be scrubbed off to keep the containers porous.

Clay pots can be quite heavy when planted. And several hundred plants in clay pots could be quite a load on your greenhouse bench.

Plastic pots. Greenhouse gardeners seem to be using plastic pots more and more. They are easy to clean, lightweight even when watered, and available in a wide range of colors, shapes, and sizes.

Plastic containers are nonporous, a condition that could create a watering problem. The pot can't absorb any excess moisture or permit air circulation through its sides. But there's another side of the coin: because watered plants grown in plastic pots remain moist longer than plants in porous pots, they will need watering less frequently; this feature could be a real lifesaver to the busy greenhouse gardener. Some plastic containers have wide slits for drainage holes; for crocking, use a thin layer of stones or pebbles instead of pot shards.

The old art of bench gardening

Though it has become less common in recent years, some greenhouses contain deep benches that hold soil and are used as very large flats. Seeds or plants are grown directly in the soil. This type of greenhouse gardening is best used for growing plants from seeds (see pages 56-57), cuttings (see pages 58-59), or seedlings of the same plants because all the plants in the bench will receive the same care.

Benches, which should be sturdy and watertight, are usually made of metal or of wood that is lined with plastic.

Unless you are an expert gardener, this type of gardening could present problems. All plants are subject to the same care, and a mistake will affect them all. Any soil-borne disease will infect all the plants. And a severe case of damping off (see page 94) could be devastating.

Many large commercial growers are no longer using their large benches, having found that smaller flats or individual seed trays are equally profitable and much less work. The soil in these benches must be changed or sterilized periodically—

ideally after each use—and this can be messy, time-consuming, and costly.

Watering: important outdoors and in

Providing water for your plants is one of the most important duties you will perform. Plants need water to survive, but just the right amount—too much water can be as damaging as too little water.

Most greenhouse gardeners water with a hose or a large watering can. Whichever method you use, a spray or mist nozzle is recommended because it breaks the force of the water. A strong jet of water from a hose or watering can can gouge a hole in the soil and expose plant roots.

The water itself should be at room temperature. Cold water can severely damage plants and foliage. Let your hose run for a few minutes until the water has warmed up. If providing warm water directly is impossible, keep a large container—a plastic garbage can or a barrel—filled for your daily waterings. Be sure to keep this container covered when not in use, as it could become a breeding ground for mosquitoes or flies.

Never use softened water on your plants. Most outdoor faucets are not attached to the water softener and can be safely tapped.

Some greenhouse gardeners use a drip irrigation system. These systems allow you to water many plants at the same time and can be effective if a large number of your plants have the same watering needs. You install plastic or

Flexible-spout filler faucet (*commonly used in service stations*) *needs only squeeze of thumb to turn on; is good for greenhouse use because it doesn't waste water or leave a wet trail between pots.*

metal pipe along your benches and then drill holes in the pipe at intervals. For one system, you install in the holes spikelike inserts that let the water drop, bubble, or squirt out into plant containers. Another system, slightly different, makes use of thin plastic tubes (called "spaghetti hose") that run from the pipe into the plant container. The thin tubes will need to be anchored inside the pots. You can automate this system with a timing device that turns the water on for a certain length of time each day, or you can operate it manually. Both of these watering systems are made by several manufacturers and marketed under different names, but if you describe what you want at a nursery or garden center, you should be able to locate one.

The majority of greenhouse gardeners still water each plant individually. This is probably the safest way to water, especially if you grow many different kinds of plants, for that way each plant will be given individual attention and hopefully will be watered properly.

Plants need "vitamins" too

Plants grown in containers will need to be fertilized, since their roots are confined and can't search out the nutrients they need in the ground. Once the nutrients in the potting mix are used up, your plant is stranded. It's up to you to replenish these nutrients by applying fertilizer.

Plant fertilizers usually contain three main ingredients: nitrogen, phosphorus, and potassium or potash. Some fertilizers also include needed trace elements. The ratio of these three ingredients is usually indicated on the label by three numbers, such as 5-10-5 or 18-20-16. The first number refers to the percentage of nitrogen, which stimulates leaf growth and helps leaves maintain a rich green color. The second number indicates the percentage of phosphorus, which promotes sturdy cell structure and healthy root growth and aids in flower and fruit production. The third number refers to the percentage of potassium, which aids plants in normal plant functions and development. Many fertilizers are formulated for specific types of plants. Read the labels carefully to make sure the fertilizers should be used on the plants you grow in your greenhouse.

Fertilizers come in several forms: liquids, powders, tablets, and capsules. Most of these fertilizers are to be dissolved and diluted in water before you apply them.

If you attach a siphon-proportioner to the watering hose, you can put the siphon into a container of prepared fertilizer and fertilize your plants while you water them. A watering can is another way to apply liquid fertilizer.

Tablets and slow-release capsules are placed on the soil surface or scratched into the soil itself. Slow-release fertilizers allow nutrients to be slowly dissolved during normal waterings over a period of time. Tablets and slow-release capsules can be great timesavers in the greenhouse, and you won't have to fertilize as often.

In a greenhouse where you're dealing with a large number of plants, it's a good idea to keep accurate watering and fertilizing records. These records will be invaluable if you must leave your greenhouse in someone else's care. And you can check to see if your prize geranium actually does need more fertilizer, or if it has another problem.

How do you know how much fertilizer to apply? Follow the instructions on the label, or to be on the safe side, dilute the solution even more than is recommended. Again, be familiar with your plants' needs; then you can be sure you're caring for them properly.

Greenhousekeeping

Your greenhouse, like everything else, needs a periodic cleaning. This is the time to scrutinize your plant collection and discard specimens that really aren't performing well. It's also the time to make sure all your equipment is working properly.

If possible, clear out the greenhouse completely and wash it down. Scrub off any moss or mildew that has formed, and clean off the walls and roof, both inside and out, to provide maximum light. If your cleaning time is in the fall, this is also a good time to remove any whitewash that has survived the summer rains. And you can be sure the greenhouse is prepared for winter.

With the greenhouse empty, you can rearrange the plants in a neat, orderly fashion. This should also make you aware of any diseased or pest-infested plants. Treat them before you return them to the greenhouse (see pages 92-94), or if they're too far gone, discard them.

Once the greenhouse has been cleaned, you'll be surprised at how nice it can look.

Plastic strips *of inflated bubbles (normally used as packing material) are pressed against greenhouse glass walls and roof; act as insulation. Strips are held to glass by condensation from humidity in greenhouse.*

If you need to winterize...

With our current energy problems, winterizing the greenhouse takes on new meaning, no matter what climate you live in. Not only will you prepare for winter, you will almost certainly try to find ways to conserve heat and cut down on your energy needs.

Before the first frost, check for—and repair—any broken or torn wall coverings. Make sure the doors and vents shut tightly and have a good seal. Replace any caulk or seal that has worn out. And make sure your various climatic equipment systems are working efficiently.

Some new ways to conserve heat are under experiment by concerned greenhouse gardeners. They have found that double layers of wall and ceiling materials create a pocket of dead air between the two layers and serve as insulation. One way to create this insulation is to attach soft plastic to the frame inside the greenhouse. Another way is to use a soft plastic packing material that has rows of inflated bubbles as a second layer. Cut the packing material into strips to fit your wall panels and simply press the bubble side of the material against the glass or rigid plastic windows. Most greenhouses have enough humidity in the air and condensation on the walls to cause this packing material to adhere.

Soft plastic covers corrugated fiberglass walls, roof of this greenhouse, forming insulation pocket of dead air between. Electrical switches operate fans, lights, heater.

Head-start gardening: grow plants from seed

Starting seeds in your greenhouse will give you a jump on the growing season. You will have vigorous seedlings ready to plant out in your garden as soon as warm weather arrives.

Seeds of annuals and vegetables are the two types most commonly started in greenhouses, though almost any type can be. Since all annuals and most vegetables mature, bloom, and go to seed in a relatively short time—from the last spring frost to the first fall frost in many areas—it's helpful to have the seedlings ready to go into the garden when planting time arrives, so they can benefit from as long a growing season as possible. You can also force annuals into bloom out of season in a greenhouse (see pages 80-81).

Seeds can be purchased in a variety of stores, including nurseries, grocery stores, hardware stores, and department stores. In addition to regular seeds, you'll probably be able to buy seed tape, a dissolvable material that has seeds evenly spaced throughout its length. When the tape is buried in soil and watered, the coating around the seeds deteriorates, permitting the seeds to sprout.

Since nursery flats accommodate from 60 to 80 plants each, they are best for large-scale production. For smaller

Seeds come in many sizes—from almost microscopic to pebble size. Here, tiny rhododendron seeds contrast with single Kentucky Wonder string bean seed, all shown in palm of hand.

quantities plant in a heated propagating tray (see page 43), half-flats, clay pots, or seed pans (shallow pots) ; all containers should have drainage. If containers have been used in the past, sterilize them (see page 52) before you plant in them. Scrub the insides with a mixture of bleach and water and leave the containers in the sun for several days to kill any fungus spores that may lurk in tiny openings.

Either a commercial potting soil or a mixture of equal parts topsoil, sand, and peat moss make good planting mixes. Line flats with newspaper to prevent soil from washing out between the boards, and then slash the paper several times to permit water to pass through. Fill the containers with soil and tap them on the ground to settle the contents; add more soil if there's room. Now you're ready to plant.

Very fine seeds should be sprinkled over the surface of the soil; it might help to mix them with a small amount of sand, which acts as a carrier. Larger seeds and seed tape can be planted in shallow furrows; these will vary in depth according to the size of the seed. Place loose seeds in the furrows by hand or carefully shake them from the seed package. Sprinkle soil over the newly planted seeds and smooth it with the palm of your hand, pressing gently to firm the soil. Label each flat to avoid confusion.

Water the soil gently with a rain-type watering can or a fine mist from a hose. Keep the pressure low so the seeds won't be disturbed.

Cover the watered containers with damp newspaper and put them in a warm spot away from direct sunlight and drafts. Keep the planting mixture moist, but not soaking wet. When the first seedlings appear, remove the newspaper covering and put the containers in full light, but not in direct sunlight.

Transplant the seedlings to individual pots or to their permanent spots in the garden as soon as two sets of leaves show. If not transplanted promptly, the seedlings may get spindly and be stunted.

If you have leftover seeds, store them, well labeled, in a dark, dry place. Many seeds have a low germination rate when kept from one season to the next; unless you have rare specimens it's probably best to buy fresh seeds each year.

Compartmented flat *uses strips of metal for dividers (heavy paper works as well) to separate an assortment of plant seeds. A prepared soil mixture is a must.*

How seeds sprout

Have you ever wondered how a seed gets its start? The process is called germination, and when it begins, life within the seed begins, too. Germination depends on the seed's being planted at the proper depth and having in the soil the right combination of water, air, and temperature.

Seeds vary greatly in size—some are as large as pebbles; others are of dustlike smallness. Within a protective coat, each seed contains an embryo plant and a supply of stored food to start the young plant on its way. It is these stored foods that we eat in grains, peas, beans, and nuts.

When germination occurs, the seed coat splits, a rootlet starts downward, and a sprout carrying the seed leaves makes its way toward the soil surface. Seed leaves usually differ in appearance from the plant's mature leaves. As soon as the true leaves expand, usually in a day or so, the young plant can function on its own.

The preferred temperature for seed germination in the greenhouse is about 70°, day and night. A few species, though, such as cyclamen and freesias, require a lower temperature, about 60°, for prompt germination. A propagating tray (a flat wired with an electric coil heater) is a convenient way to maintain a constant soil temperature. Most nurseries carry styrofoam flats with built-in coils, or you can buy just the heating coils and install them yourself in a wooden flat, following the directions that come with the coil. Be sure that whatever container you use as a propagating tray has adequate drainage; it's better for the plants and safer for use with an electric coil.

A lightweight, sterile soil is best for starting seeds; delicate root tips can readily penetrate a light potting mix, and sterilization of the soil prevents weed growth and eliminates a fungus that causes damping off. Damping off attacks the tender stalks of seedlings just above the soil level, causing them to topple (see page 94).

Depth of planting is related to seed size. Except for very small ones that are scattered over the soil surface, seeds are generally planted at a depth two to four times their diameter. Be careful not to plant too deep; most failures result from the seed's being buried alive. Also avoid sowing too thickly, as this creates such problems as weak seedlings and difficulty in transplanting. After you've planted the flat, water it well; the soil should never be allowed to totally dry out during the germination period.

Between growing seasons, set up your propagating tray and prepare the soil. For an armchair adventure, try going through seed catalogues. The variety of seeds they offer will intrigue you and kindle anticipation of the coming spring. With your propagating tray ready, you can get right to work as soon as planting time arrives.

Plastic-covered seed tape (water soluble) is cut to fit length of flat, then covered with prepared soil mix; bed is slowly soaked.

Seed furrows are made with ruler (your finger is also a good tool) after soil mix is leveled. Place seeds in furrows and cover with soil.

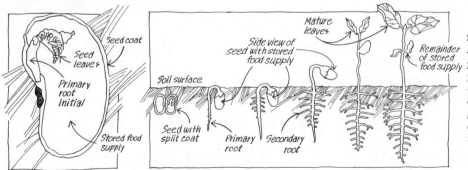

Seed development begins with bean seed (at left) that contains embryo plant. Seed coat will soon split, allowing primary root initial to lengthen and develop into main root of seedling. Stored food supply keeps seedling growing until mature leaves develop and plant begins to manufacture its own food.

The pleasures of growing plants from cuttings

Here is a common gardening dilemma: your neighbor has gorgeous geraniums that are just the right shade for your patio, but you've never seen them in a nursery. Or you visit a friend who has a splendid fuchsia, but she can't remember what variety it is. What can you do? Take cuttings and grow your own plants.

Starting plants from cuttings is an economical way to increase your plant collection. Also, plants grown from cuttings will be just like their parents, whereas seeds may develop into plants very different from their parents.

New plants: softwood cuttings

You can take these new-growth cuttings from late spring well into summer, beginning as soon as spring growth is firm and sturdy. In choosing cuttings, look for normal healthy growth; avoid both fat and spindly branches. Softwood cuttings root best if you can snap them off cleanly from the parent plant. If they crush or bend, the wood is too old. If new leaves are still forming at the tip, the branch is too young for a cutting. Keep all cuttings cool and damp (not wet) until you can plant them.

To start softwood cuttings, fill your propagation tray (see photo on page 43) with a mixture of one part clean, sharp river sand (never use sea sand) and one part premoistened peat moss. Place an opened container of rooting hormone powder next to the propagation tray. Take the cuttings, one at a time, from their moist wrapping and make a clean, slanting cut with a razor blade or sharp knife just below a leaf or bud.

Strip off lower leaves so only the stem will be buried in the rooting medium. If the remaining upper leaves are very large, snip off about half of each leaf with scissors. Dip the stem in the hormone powder and tap it gently to remove any excess. With a pencil make a hole in the rooting mixture and set in the cutting; firm the soil around the stem.

Softwood cuttings will root much more easily if you provide bottom heat, keeping the temperature between 70° and 80° in the rooting medium. Place the cuttings out of direct sunlight where the atmosphere around the leaves is moist and warm—so the upper parts of the cutting don't dry out. If your greenhouse isn't humid enough, you can put a plastic bag over the cuttings to retain moisture (remove it for an hour or so once a day to get rid of any condensation).

Here are some plants you might like to take softwood cuttings from: azalea, candytuft, chrysanthemum, delphinium, fuchsia, geranium (including ivy geranium and pelargonium), ivy, oleander, star jasmine, and wisteria.

New plants: hardwood cuttings

Certain deciduous shrubs and trees can be grown from cuttings taken in autumn, after the leaves have fallen but before the first frost. Cut off the tip of a selected branch at a point where it becomes about pencil thick. Discard the tip and cut off the next 6 to 9-inch section that includes at least two leaf buds; the end near the trunk should be cut on a slant just below a bud. Be sure to label each cutting, then store them upright in a container of sand until spring; during this time the cut ends will callus over.

Since these cuttings may take up to a year to root, you'll want to start them in an out-of-the-way spot where they won't be disturbed; under a bench in the greenhouse would be a good place. Apply rooting powder the same way you would to a softwood cutting (see page 59). Then set the cuttings in rooting medium (half sand, half peat moss) up to the upper pair of buds, spacing the cuttings about 4 inches apart.

When the cuttings have rooted and show enough sturdy growth, you can move them to their permanent spot. Keep them shaded until they become established and begin to grow.

Try making hardwood cuttings from these plants: deutzia, forsythia, grape, kolkwitzia, philadelphus, and weigela.

New plants: leaf cuttings

Some plants, like the piggy-back (*Tolmiea*) or strawberry geranium (*Saxifraga*), wave their offspring invitingly, tempting you to pot them individually. Other plants—most gesneriads and begonias, for example—don't appear as eager to increase their numbers, yet they also will root readily from leaf cuttings. Succulent or fleshy-leafed plants are best for this type of propagation.

With a razor blade, cleanly cut firm, healthy leaves from the parent plant. Hormone powders aren't needed for these cuttings.

There are three ways to root leaves in a sand and peat mixture. Gesneriad leaves can be buried in a rooting medium up to the leaf blade; firm the medium around them. Don't let the leaves touch each other as they could rot. Long, thin succulent leaves, like those of mother-in-law's tongue,

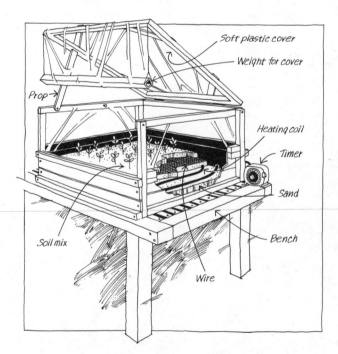

Propagating box *made from scrap lumber is used to start seedlings, cuttings. Timer controls heating coil.*

can be cut into sections about 3 to 4 inches long, set into the medium about 1 to 2 inches deep, and rooted in the same manner. Begonia plants can be started from leaf pieces that include vein sections. Either insert a piece of the leaf about an inch into the medium or slash across the veins and lay the leaf on top of the medium; hold it securely in place with pebbles.

Leaf cuttings shouldn't be rooted where the humidity is too high—diseases can infect succulent leaves easily in damp conditions. To stimulate root formation and growth, water the rooting medium with a mixture of vitamin B-1 and water after leaf cuttings are inserted (follow label directions for proportions). When new growth appears you can plant the cuttings in small pots.

Starting new plants from cuttings can be very fulfilling. But don't overdo it; it's easy to be completely overrun by tiny new plants in small containers.

1. **Before you start,** *gather strong, healthy cutting, rooting hormone powder, punch, pruning shears, knife, cutting block, pot filled with rooting mix.*

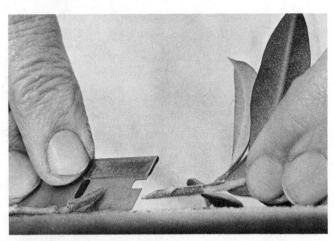

2. **Use razor blade** *or sharp knife to make long, slanted end cut, exposing cambium layer of stem.*

3. **Gently remove leaves** *from bottom two-thirds of cutting to lessen danger of stem rot from buried leaves.*

4. **Far left:** *Dip cut end of specimen into rooting hormone powder to speed rooting process. Shake off excess powder.*

5. **Punch hole** *in potting mix, then insert cutting (left). With fingers, gently firm soil around base of cutting.*

Vegetables all year – under glass

Food from your greenhouse, as well as flowers, can be more than just a dream. Many vegetables will grow and produce inside the greenhouse the year around. If your space is limited, you can grow cherry tomatoes and other small-space vegetables. But if you can spare the room, you can have tomatoes, cucumbers, and other vegetables of regular size the year around.

The type of greenhouse you have (see pages 82-86 on the cool and warm greenhouses) will determine the type of vegetables you can grow. Lettuce, radishes, and other cool season plants like the cool greenhouse atmosphere; tomatoes, cucumbers, and other hot weather vegetables, though, need a warm greenhouse.

Whichever vegetables you decide to grow, there are certain things you should be aware of. Most vegetables, especially vines, need a great deal of space. Some gardeners train the vines to grow up support posts to save space. Whatever your situation, you need to provide the necessary space if you're to be successful. Vegetables grow best in raised beds constructed on the greenhouse floor; use redwood or cedar frames and a lightweight soil mix.

Large tomato plants *reach into rafters of this glass-and-wood greenhouse. Vegetables, herbs grow in raised beds along sides.*

Cucumber vine twists *around center pipe supports inside glass-and-wood greenhouse. This special "English hothouse" cucumber grows in wooden container on top of bench.*

As the vegetables mature, you will need to provide support for them. You may also need to hand-pollinate those plants that have flowers, as your greenhouse may lack the necessary insect population. Do this in one of three ways: use a soft camel's-hair brush on each of the blossom clusters to move the pollen from flower to flower; gently shake the plant; or use a fan.

Lath strips *are placed over pipe frame to give temporary shade to lettuce, other tender vegetables. Tomatoes, other sun-loving plants remain exposed to sunlight.*

Keep a careful eye on your vegetable plants for any possible problems; the plants may invite unwanted pests or diseases into the greenhouse. If you do find an infested plant, spray it to keep the problem under control. When the plants are beginning to decline, remove them. Weak or old annual plants invite trouble.

You can keep a continuous cycle of vegetables going throughout the year if you plant new seeds periodically. When you remove old spent vegetables, you'll have new seedlings to replace them.

If you have a cool greenhouse, you may want to try growing lettuce, radishes, and herbs. And if you have lots of room, try rhubarb.

In a warm greenhouse, you can grow tomatoes, cucumbers, green peppers, and if you can spare the room, melons.

Cucumber vines *are trained against greenhouse wall with twine, wire.*

The world of Lilliputian vegetables

If you'd like to grow some novel but useful plants, try miniature vegetables. Their smallness is appealing where space is a problem—frequently the case in a greenhouse—and they have other practical advantages, too. Miniature vegetables are usually ready to harvest sooner than regular-size ones, and single people or small families may find them more convenient. Because most miniatures are small enough to finish at one meal, you don't have leftover vegetables cluttering up the refrigerator.

Most of these Lilliputian delicacies can be sown at almost any time of year in the greenhouse. Inland gardeners would be wise to wait until fall to start cool season crops such as lettuce, cabbage, and (in some areas) peas—then it's easier to keep a greenhouse cool and avoid bolting (having the plants go to seed prematurely).

Many miniature vegetable varieties are available. Park Seed Co., Greenwood, SC 29647 has the above three vegetables plus cantaloupe, carrots, cucumbers, eggplant, sweet corn, tomatoes, and watermelon. W. Atlee Burpee Co., 6350 Rutland Avenue, Riverside, CA 92502 has seeds for "Tiny Tim" tomatoes and "New Hampshire Midget" watermelon.

Plant miniature vegetables in containers or in a propagating tray. They'll do well in a porous, fast-draining soil mix. You can use a commercial mix or make your own with one part garden loam, one part river sand, and one part leaf mold or peat moss. To maintain steady growth, feed your miniature plants weekly with properly diluted fish emulsion, or use a timed-release fertilizer that provides nutrients for the entire growing season.

When watering, avoid wetting the vegetables' leaves. Damp leaves coupled with the high humidity in most greenhouses increase the chances of mildew developing.

Whether you want to raise only a few vegetables for an occasional snack while working in your greenhouse, or enough to supply your table and give some away, try growing these miniatures. They're easy, compact, unique—and just plain fun to grow.

'Golden Midget' sweet corn *ears average 4 inches in length. Plants grow to about 2½ feet tall. Corn is harvested some 60 days after planting.*

'Tom Thumb' lettuce *has tiny head (about tennis ball size), is exceptionally crisp and sweet.*

'Little Finger' carrots *grow to 3 inches long, are ready to eat 2 months after planting.*

Hydroponics in the greenhouse

If you ever have a yen to try a different style of gardening, consider hydroponics. Also known as water culture, aquaculture, and soilless gardening, hydroponics is a method of growing plants in a nutrient solution without soil. The plants, which are usually grown in shallow trays, are supported by an inert medium such as gravel.

Your greenhouse is an ideal place for a hydroponic garden. Temperature and humidity can be maintained in the growing range that's best for your plants, creating a nearly perfect environment.

Hydroponic gardening has ancient roots. A scientific approach to water culture was first tried in 1699 for the purpose of studying plant nutrition. More recently, during World War II, hydroponic gardens were set up in several remote areas to grow fresh produce to help feed soldiers stationed there. Since then, hydroponic techniques have been improved and simplified enough to make water culture attractive to home gardeners.

Why are individuals setting up hydroponic gardens? There are many reasons, including novelty, high crop yield, automatic watering and feeding, and the freedom of having no cultivating, weeding, mulching, or soil-borne diseases to contend with. Hydroponic gardens can be located almost anywhere, as long as there's electricity to run the equipment. The trays take up little space. And since nutrients are delivered to the roots, rather than the roots ranging through the soil to find nutriment, less space is needed for a hydroponic garden than a conventional garden.

A few basic pieces of equipment are necessary to start your hydroponic garden: trays, growing medium, pipes, valves, and a storage tank for the solution. To have an automatic system, you'll also need a pump and a timer. The equipment can be purchased as a kit or piece by piece; instructions are generally included.

A tray is the first thing you'll need to set up a hydroponic garden. Kits usually include trays, or you can use almost anything that will support a bed of growing medium 8 to 9 inches deep. Avoid galvanized iron or tin trays, though; the zinc in the metal can poison your plants. Brick, fiberglass, redwood, plastic, and concrete are good container materials. Some may need to be lined with plastic film or fiberglass and resin to keep them from leaking. Position the trays before you fill them with the medium, which can be heavy.

Fill the trays with 8 to 9 inches of medium; be sure to leave at least an inch between the top of the medium and the top of the tray. Some examples of growing media are pea gravel, wood chips, crushed brick, perlite, glass marbles, and sand. The growing medium's function is to support the plants and retain moisture while letting the roots breathe. Though gravel is a bit heavy, it's the most popular growing medium. Pea gravel, 1/4 to 3/8 inch in diameter, meets the requirements for a good medium—it supports plants adequately, yet is porous enough that nutrient flow isn't blocked and roots can breathe.

Next, position the nutrient storage tank; it should be lower than the grow tray so the solution can flow through the tray and return to the tank by gravity flow. (Either elevate the growing tray or sink the storage tank; see drawings on facing page.) The tank can be almost anything from a commercial fiberglass reservoir to a plastic-lined wooden box. You should now connect the pipe and valve

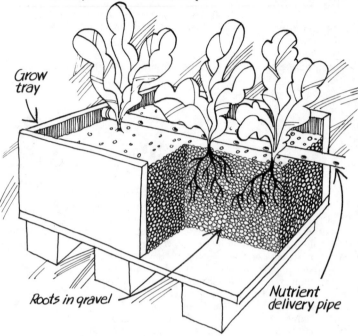

Hydroponic grow tray *contains pea gravel which supports young plants, allows nutrient solution to circulate freely. Gravel layer is 8 to 9 inches deep.*

Grow tray

Roots in gravel

Nutrient delivery pipe

system; PVC (polyvinyl chloride) pipe is easy to work with and won't be corroded by the nutrient solution. You'll need three pipes: 1) a pipe from the tank to the grow tray to deliver the solution to the roots, 2) a return pipe, and 3) a pipe to the outside of the greenhouse to dispose of the tired nutrient solution.

Follow the manufacturer's instructions for installation and operation of the pipe system, pump, timer, and other equipment. Directions may vary among kits. Be sure all electric equipment is UL approved; this is especially important since water is involved. You should check the building codes in your area for any possible restrictions, too.

Now that all the equipment is set up, you're ready to plant. Almost any plant that can be cultivated can be grown hydroponically; vegetables, annuals, and even bulbs are popular examples. There are three methods for getting plants started in a hydroponic garden: planting seeds directly in the medium, starting seeds in compressed peat pellets, and buying nursery seedlings.

Large seeds can be planted directly in the growing medium or started in peat pellets. Small seeds should be started in peat pellets; otherwise they could wash through any openings in the growing medium and fail to germinate. Try to use peat pellets that expand when put in water; these are surrounded by a thin net that holds them together. When seedlings are up 2 to 4 inches, plant the entire pellet in the growing medium. Nursery seedlings are convenient for immediate planting, but they will have to adjust to the new watering system, and they can occasionally carry disease into the greenhouse. Start plenty of seedlings; you can pull some out later if necessary.

It's best to use plain water (without nutrients) in your grow tray until the plants are established and growing. Then, introduce the nutrient solution gradually so plants won't be shocked. The solution should be circulated through the grow tank twice a day—never at night and preferably not during the hottest part of the day, because plants can't use nutrients efficiently at these times. After the tank is filled, the solution slowly (over a period of 2 to 3 hours) drains back into the storage tank, allowing the roots to breathe again. Until you become an experienced hydroponic gardener, it's best to start with a commercial nutrient mix that contains the essential elements in the proper amounts.

It's a good idea to keep notes on what happens in your hydroponic garden for future reference; it would be frustrating to forget which tomato variety copiously produced fruit 4 inches in diameter.

Look in the Yellow Pages under "Hydroponic Equipment and Supplies" for information on where to get kits, fixtures, and instructions. Give this unique type of gardening a try; it takes little space and time, and it can be very rewarding.

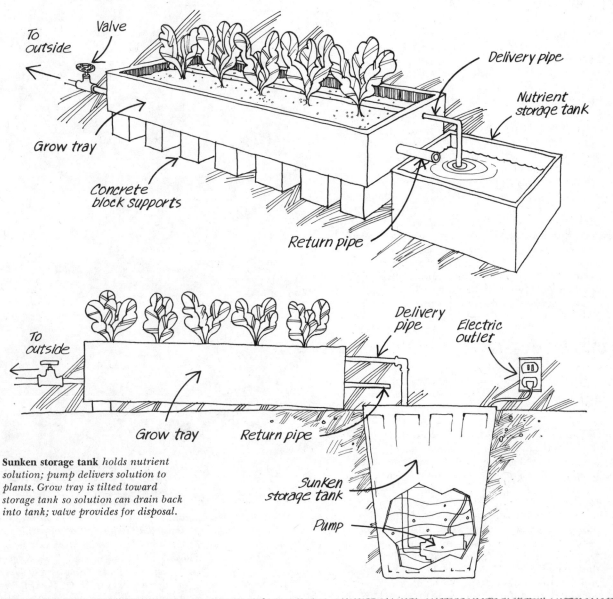

Elevated grow tray *allows nutrient solution to drain into lower storage tank. Gardener opens valve for easy disposal of exhausted nutrient solution.*

To outside

Valve

Delivery pipe

Nutrient storage tank

Grow tray

Concrete block supports

Return pipe

Delivery pipe

Electric outlet

To outside

Grow tray

Return pipe

Sunken storage tank

Pump

Sunken storage tank *holds nutrient solution; pump delivers solution to plants. Grow tray is tilted toward storage tank so solution can drain back into tank; valve provides for disposal.*

Commonly grown specialty plants

Many gardeners become partial to a certain group of plants, and before they're even aware of what's happening, they have acquired a sizeable collection in that one special plant family. The plant groups we've selected are those most commonly grown by greenhouse gardeners.

Many of these plants can be grown as house plants, it's true. But grown inside a greenhouse, they'll thrive! A greenhouse environment provides optimum conditions for growing most plants—controlled temperatures, maximum light, and high humidity. And as a collector, you'll enjoy having the plants all in one place.

Orchids – kings of the roost

Orchids are the true monarchs of the greenhouse. Many gardeners think of "orchid" and "greenhouse" almost as synonymous terms, and orchids are probably the most widely grown greenhouse plants. The orchid family is large and diverse, with countless species from all parts of the world.

A long history is credited to orchids. Confucius, in ancient China, described orchids as "flowers of great refinement to be held in high esteem." And the Greek philosopher Theophrastus, a contemporary of Plato and Aristotle, first called them by the name *orchis,* from which the term orchid was derived. In the late 1700s, plant explorers began collecting orchids from the tropical regions of the New World. And the orchid has been grown for purely ornamental purposes ever since.

Most orchids fall into two basic groups: the epiphytes and the terrestrials. Epiphytic orchids grow on the bark of trees, getting water from the rain and nutrients from the air and any organic matter that collects around their roots by chance. Terrestrial orchids grow like most normal plants, with their roots in the soil. It is important to know which type your orchids are, because they need to be grown differently.

Specialized needs

Because growing orchids requires very specialized growing conditions, many gardeners have the impression they are tricky to grow. But if you meet their needs, they will perform admirably.

Not all orchids can be treated alike. There are two types of growth in orchid plants: sympodial and monopodial. Plants with a monopodial growth habit become taller each year, with new growth emerging at the tip of the stem (see photo at top right). Orchids with sympodial growth— the most prevalent type of orchid growth—form each year's new growth from the base of the previous season's growth. Sympodial growth is characterized by a creeping stem, called a rhizome, from which roots go downward and the leaves and flowers grow upward (see photo at bottom right).

Most of the sympodial orchids have pseudobulbs, thickened stems that store nutrients and water so the plants can survive seasons of drought. In fact, sympodial-type orchids need a drying out period between waterings. Monopodial-

An example of monopodial growth, *this orchid's central stem (top above) grows in an upward direction on top of previous season's growth. Aerial roots and flower stalks also come from plant's central stem.* **Below:** *Sympodial growth is typical of the majority of orchids. New growth originates from base of previous year's growth, traveling in a horizontal direction, then upward. Rhizome or creeping stem forms roots that grow downward and leaves and flower stalks that grow upward.*

type orchids, though, require more attention to their watering needs; they should not be allowed to dry out, as they have no means of water storage. These two types of growth are pictured at right.

Specific requirements for growing orchids are listed below. Since different orchids have different needs, you should be able to find several species you can grow in your present greenhouse conditions.

Light. A good rule of thumb is to give your orchids as much sun as they can take without burning the leaves. Most healthy orchids have light green leaves; lush dark green plants probably won't bloom. Brown spots on the leaves and pseudobulbs indicate too much sun.

Many greenhouse gardeners like white or clear rigid plastic roof coverings for their orchids: because light coming through the plastic panels is modified into a soft, even light, the possibility of sunburn damage is lessened.

Temperature. Many orchids can be successfully grown in a warm greenhouse. They prefer daytime temperatures from 70° to 85° with a drop of 10° to 15° at night. The drop in the nighttime temperature is important, because it slows down transpiration (loss of moisture through the leaves) and speeds up growth. Some orchids need cooler nights to set flower buds.

Cool growing orchids—such as odontoglossums and miltonias—will be happier in temperature ranges about 10° less, both day and night (the cool greenhouse is discussed on pages 82-83). If you have a warm greenhouse (see pages 84-85 for more information) and want to grow some cool-temperature orchids, don't despair. Most warm greenhouses contain areas where the temperature is cool enough to accommodate these orchids.

Humidity. Since most orchids come from the tropics, they like high humidity. A good humidity level in the greenhouse is between 40 and 60 percent with good air circulation. The higher the daytime temperatures, the more humidity you should provide; high temperatures without corresponding levels of humidity can cause plants to transpire rapidly and wilt. If you plan to specialize in the orchid family, your greenhouse should be equipped with a humidifier (see page 34 for information) and a hygrometer (see page 35). Hygrometers measure the amount of moisture present in the air. As temperatures lower in the evening, so should the humidity as a precaution against disease organisms.

Ventilation. A very important consideration in growing orchids is ventilation. In the wilds, they constantly receive fresh, moving air. In your greenhouse, you can keep the air moving with circulating fans (see pages 33-34). Orchids don't like drafts, though, so make sure the fans don't blow directly onto the benches that hold the plants. Greenhouse benches should have slots or other regularly spaced openings so that air is free to move around the plant roots. Several bench styles that promote good air circulation are pictured on pages 40-41.

Containers and potting mixes. The main requirement for an orchid container is large drainage holes or slots. Because ventilation is needed around the plant roots, excess water must not accumulate in the bottom of the container. Clay pots and plastic pots are common choices.

Plastic pots are generally preferred for orchids grown in the greenhouse. They hold moisture inside the potting mix over a much longer period of time than clay pots, and they're lightweight and easy to move around.

Favorite epiphytic orchid potting mediums are fir bark and osmunda fiber. Fir bark is sold as chunks of bark, graded according to size. Smaller grades are used for seedlings and miniature plants, medium grades for plants to 30 inches tall, and larger grades for large plants that prefer an open mix. Osmunda fiber is the aerial roots from two types of ferns. Unlike fir bark, it contains some nutrients, so orchids grown in it require less fertilizer. You will need to soak the fiber overnight before using it. Osmunda fiber is usually the more expensive of the two and may be harder to locate.

Terrestrial orchids may require a sturdier, more nutritious growing medium: chopped osmunda, leaf mold, and small-grade fir bark in equal parts form a good potting mix.

Watering and fertilizing. There is no single rule for watering orchids. Different plants need different amounts of water. The best advice concerning water is to familiarize yourself with your individual plants and their watering needs. When watering orchids, always use tepid water at about 60° to 70°.

Fertilizing orchids is easy, even for the beginner. Commercial orchid fertilizers are available for most types of plants. Read the label carefully and follow instructions exactly.

Cattleya orchid *has white flowers with colored lips. Cattleyas need lots of light, high humidity, and a warm greenhouse.*

Graceful phalaenopsis *enjoy strong filtered light from translucent fiberglass roof. Arching flower stalks may need to be supported with wire or wooden stakes.*

Miltonia hybrid *is nicknamed "pansy orchid" because its flower shape is similar to that of the pansy. Individual flowers grow up to 4 inches wide, come in many colors and markings. Plant has long and graceful light green leaves.*

These orchids will do well

The following paragraphs list some of the most widely grown orchids. These orchids are considered relatively easy to grow; a few of them are more difficult, but they have some outstanding characteristics that make them worthy of the extra effort. Unless otherwise stated, all these orchids will thrive in a warm greenhouse environment.

Aerides. Epiphytic orchids from tropical Asia, aerides can grow very tall. They have no pseudobulbs. Closely set, fragrant, waxy flowers grow on pendant flower spikes. They require a lot of water during spring and summer, less during the remaining months. Aerides prefer bright light.

Angraecum. These epiphytic orchids from Asia and Sri Lanka bloom in winter. Starlike white or greenish white flowers appear on long, curved stems. Keep potting mix moist all year except in fall; then allow plants to dry out between waterings. Grow these orchids in bright light.

Bifrenaria. Native to Brazil, these epiphytic orchids have large, showy flowers, angled pseudobulbs, and dark green, leathery leaves. They like sun or bright light. After blooming, bifrenaria orchids should be rested without water for about a month.

Brassavola. These epiphytic orchids, native to tropical America, have large, spiderlike, white or greenish white flowers. The flowers may appear singly or in clusters. During their growing season, give them a great deal of water and sun. Reduce humidity during their dormant season.

Brassia. Here is a group of large epiphytic plants found from Mexico to Brazil and Peru. Evergreen leaves rise from plump pseudobulbs. The flower spikes hold many fragrant blooms, usually during the summer months. These plants are sun lovers and need warmth (over 60°) and water all year.

Cattleya. Epiphytic orchids native to tropical America, these plants are the most popular and best known of the orchids. Their showy flowers are widely used in corsages. The plants have pseudobulbs and are available with flowers in a wide range of colors. They like warm nighttime temperatures (60°), relatively high humidity (50-60 percent), and good light. Let the potting mix dry out between waterings and feed plants about every 2 weeks during their growing season.

Coelogyne. These epiphytic orchids grow throughout India, Malaysia, and New Guinea. Their leaves are normally dark green; flowers, usually small, are in shades of brown, cream, beige, or green. Coelogyne orchids prefer a shady location.

Dendrobium. Native to India, Burma, Sri Lanka, China, Japan, and Australia, this is one of the largest orchid groups. There are five different growth habits with different needs:

1) Pseudobulb types need abundant watering until leaves mature. Then let plants rest without water to encourage buds; after flowering, potting mix should be kept dry for 8 weeks.

2) Evergreen cane types need lots of water except for a month immediately after flowering. In the fall give them coolish nights (55°) to encourage budding.

(Continued on next page)

Paphiopedilum orchids *have flowers with lacquered or waxy appearing textures, often look more artificial than real. They are known by common name "lady's slipper orchid."*

White phalaenopsis flowers *have intricate lip structures that are often colored. Graceful shape resembles a moth in flight, earning nickname "moth orchid."*

3) Deciduous cane types need a great deal of heat and water during summer until leaves mature. Then stop watering for 6 to 8 weeks to encourage buds. When foliage falls off, move plant to a sunny but cool (45° to 50°) spot until buds begin to show; then move plants back to warmth and resume watering.

4) Evergreen phalaenopsis types need constantly warm temperatures, constant moisture, and full sun. A slight reduction of water is necessary between maturity of leaves and bud formation. These are very demanding orchids.

5) Types having black, hairy stems produce white flowers in the spring that last up to 2 months. They need even moisture, warmth, and sun all year.

Epidendrum. From tropical America, these orchids are both terrestrial and epiphytic and vary in flower form. Those with pseudobulbs need a rest after flowering. Those with cane growth need moisture all year. These orchids are generally easy to grow.

Habenaria radiata. Native to Japan, this terrestrial orchid produces a green and white flower with a large trailing spur. This plant needs constant moisture all year. It will grow in sun or partial shade and cool greenhouse temperatures. Flowers can appear at any time throughout the year. Foliage usually dies back during winter months.

Laelia. Very similar to the cattleya, these epiphytic orchids are from tropical America. The plants have pseudobulbs. Flowers are generally smaller than cattleyas, and their growing needs are the same; they may need more sun for best flowering. Immediately after flowering, withhold water until new growth appears. Let potting mix dry out between waterings.

Lycaste. Epiphytic orchids from Mexico, the West Indies, and Central and South America, these can be either deciduous or semideciduous. The long-lasting flowers are usually green, but some blooms are pink, white, yellow, or brown. These orchids need a cool greenhouse (50° to 55° at night, 10° higher during the day), no direct sun, and constant watering except for the period between flowering and the appearance of new growth.

Miltonia. Called pansy orchids because of the similarity between the two flowers, these epiphytic orchids come from Costa Rica and Brazil. They have elongated pseudobulbs with long, graceful, light green foliage that grows in a clump. Types that produce white or pink flowers marked with magenta, crimson, or yellow should be grown in a cool greenhouse. Those with yellow or white flowers marked with purple or brown need the warmer temperatures. Grow miltonias almost as you do cattleyas, except for light; these orchids require less light and no direct sun.

Odontoglossum. Grow these orchids in a cool greenhouse; they come from the foggy regions at high altitudes in the Andes Mountains of South America. Flowers of this epiphytic orchid are delicate and ruffled and come in white, yellow, brown, and pink. Plants usually have flattened pseudobulbs sheathed with small leaves. They prefer crowded conditions, so use smaller pots than normal for the size of the plant. Give them constant moisture and lots of light but no direct sun.

Oncidium. Most of these epiphytic orchids produce yellow flowers marked with brown on long flower spikes. These plants come from Mexico, Central America, the West Indies, and parts of Brazil. Some species have compressed pseudobulbs topped by one or two leaves; others are almost without bulbs. Flowers are small and numerous or large and sparse. Grow oncidiums similarly to cattleyas. They like a cool

greenhouse, much sun, and a rest period with no water for several weeks after new growth is completed.

Paphiopedilum. Sometimes sold as cypripediums, these orchids are called lady slippers because of their shape. They are native to the Old World tropics. Flowers have striking, sometimes bizarre, color combinations and a waxy, almost artificial, appearance. Foliage can be plain green on plants that bloom in winter or mottled on plants that are summer blooming. The plain-leafed varieties like a cool greenhouse, while the mottled-leafed plants like warm temperatures (60° to 65° at night and 70° to 85° during the day). They prefer good light but no direct sun. They are terrestrial and need constant moisture at their roots. They also prefer less humidity than most orchids—around 30 to 50 percent. They may be sensitive to fertilizers.

Phalaenopsis. Nicknamed the moth orchid because of the flower shape, phalaenopsis orchids come from the tropics of Asia. White and pink are the most common flower colors, but some hybrids come in yellow and multicolors. The flowers

Vanda hybrid flowers *grow to 6 inches across. This hybrid, V. 'Nellie Morley', has lavender pink spots. Vandas need much light, greater humidity than most orchids. They can't withstand temperature levels below 50°.*

appear on long, arching spikes and are quite long lasting. Plants usually bloom in late winter or spring; they like a warm greenhouse with high humidity (60 to 70 percent). They are terrestrial with no pseudobulbs but can be potted in either fir bark or osmunda. They must never dry out, and they like bright light but no direct sun. Fertilize the plants during periods of active growth only.

Stanhopea. Native to the region from Mexico through parts of South America, these epiphytic orchids produce large, fantastically shaped, short-lived, fragrant flowers in subdued colors. They should be grown in open baskets, as flower spikes may grow down through the potting mix and emerge at the base of the root ball. They like average light and careful watering during periods of growth and less water during the rest of the year; they grow under the same conditions as cattleyas. They need to be shaded from direct sun.

Vanda. Originally native to the Philippines, Malaysia, and the Himalayas, these are now grown as a commercial crop in the Hawaiian Islands. Growth habit is monopodial, and plants may eventually reach 4 feet or higher. Plants with pencillike leaves need a warm greenhouse and full sun in order to flower (artificial lights could be used; see pages 36-37). Vandas with strap-shaped leaves need less light to flower. They like lots of water, high humidity, and temperatures above 50°.

What's in a name?

Has it ever occurred to you that those long Latin words that seem difficult to spell and impossible to pronounce could be useful words to know? They can. Many plants share the same common name, and often you'll have to use the Latin name to get the exact plant you want. Because it is universally accepted, Latin was chosen as the language of scientific nomenclature.

Nomenclature was chaotic before the binomial (combination of genus and species) system was developed. Plants were named descriptively with Latin adjectives. Imagine how agonizing it would be to use a name like *Dianthus floribus solitariis, squamis calycinis subovatis brevissimus, corollis crenatis* to refer to a simple carnation—*Dianthus caryophyllus,* which means flower with a clovelike scent.

In an attempt to end the confusion, Karl von Linne, an 18th century Swedish botanist, developed a standard system for grouping and naming living creatures. Over the years, names were occasionally changed to be more fitting, and new life forms, which also required names, were discovered. The effort to classify plants took definite shape when the International Botanical Congress met in Vienna in 1905. Subsequent congresses, which meet every 5 years, modify and update the system as it becomes necessary.

Botanists have classified all plants in this orderly, ranked system that reflects the similarities among plants. Scientific plant names, which are italicized, include two or more words. The first, which is capitalized, is the genus name. The second, not capitalized, is the species name. A third word in the name indicates a variety. If the variety occurs naturally, its name is italicized, as in *Dieffenbachia picta lancifolia.* If the variety originated in and is perpetuated through cultivation, the varietal name is enclosed by single quotation marks—*Gloxinia grandiflora* 'Switzerland'. Just think of the plant's genus as a surname, the species as a first name, and the variety as a nickname.

Genus. Plant assemblages are divided into genera (plural of genus), groups of plants linked together by usually obvious, but sometimes obscure, botanical characteristics. *Paphiopedilum, Asparagus,* and *Alocasia* are examples of genera.

Species. A genus may contain only one or a great number of species. A species is a group of individual plants that are more like each other than like any other group. Species within a genus share many common features, such as leaf shape and thickness, but differ in one or more attributes.

Variety. A third word in a botanical name indicates a variety (or subspecies). Both naturally occurring and cultivated varieties retain most characteristics of the species, yet differ in some way—such as flower color or leaf size. When a group of plants is not distinctive enough to deserve a species name of its own, it is declared a variety. *Alocasia indica metallica* is an example of a variety with shiny (metallic) leaves.

You've probably noticed that after the first time a genus name is used in print it is abbreviated to the first letter. When various varieties are listed, the species name can be abbreviated, too. Some examples are *Dracaena kindtiana, D. godseffiana* and *D. g. kelleri*—three different dracaenas. These abbreviations are used for convenience and to avoid unnecessary repetition.

How does a plant get its name? And what does the name mean? Frequently, the person responsible for developing or discovering the plant is the one who names it. Classifying a plant in the correct genus requires careful study. Either the classical generic name is used or a new genus name that is descriptive of the plant is coined. Choosing a species name is more arbitrary.

The plant's discoverer may name his new find after a spouse, a friend, a colleague or someone else: *Paphiopedilum lawrenceanum* was named after a person who had the surname Lawrence. The species name may describe a characteristic of the plant: *plumosus* (as in *Asparagus plumosus*) means feathery, for example. Another common practice is to name a plant after a geographical area in which it can be found. *Indica* means of or from India or the East Indies; an example of this is *Alocasia indica.*

If, after reading this, you can't say *Anthurium scherzerianum rothschildianum* without hesitating, relax. You're perfectly normal. Understanding the principles of botanical nomenclature is the helpful thing. You can always write the name of the plant you want, and your request will be understood anywhere in the world. The merits of using Latin names—universality and avoidance of confusion—outweigh the frustrations of their pronunciations. If you let them, Latin names can become some of your best friends.

Bromeliads – offbeat and fun

Bromeliads are an unusual family of plants. They can be grown for their foliage, which may be either coarse and dull or fragile, shiny, and colorful, with or without sharp-toothed edges. Some gardeners like the flowers, which are spectacular, often bizarre, in strangely startling colors and shapes. Their lack of similarity to most other plant groups makes them very appealing to the plant collector.

Bromeliads are becoming popular house plants because of their ability to survive neglect and adverse growing conditions. You are probably familiar with the most famous member of this family, the pineapple. Bromeliads will do perfectly well inside your home, but when grown in a greenhouse under the ideal conditions—what a difference!

Bromeliads grow in many forms. The most common form is the vase or bowl shape where the leaves form a rosette with a small cup in the center that collects water. In the tropics, debris, insects, and even tiny animals fall into this cup and eventually die, providing nutrients to the plant as they decay. New leaves grow from the center of the plant, keeping the vase intact. (Since the older leaves on the outer part of the rosette die out, you can improve the plant's appearance by removing them as they dry up.) Another common form of growth is a tubular one; some billbergias grow in this manner.

Most bromeliads are epiphytes—plants that receive moisture and nourishment from the air and from debris that falls into the plant. In the wild, these plants grow on rocks or trees. A few other bromeliads are terrestrials—plants that grow in soil. And some very clever bromeliads can adapt themselves to either situation.

Easy to grow

Just because their individual botanical names have an exotic ring, these plants are expected to be difficult to grow. Luckily, their names are the most difficult thing you'll need to remember.

Light needs. These plants will produce their best bloom and leaf color when grown in good, diffused light. Hot direct sunlight can burn the tender leaves.

Temperature. Bromeliads can tolerate temperatures ranging from 130° down to zero, depending on the species, but most prefer a range between 50° and 70°. This places them into the cool greenhouse environment, though many bromeliads could adapt to a warm greenhouse.

Ventilation. Like orchids, bromeliads grow naturally in areas where the air circulates freely. Provide plenty of air circulation in the greenhouse, but be sure there are no drafts directly on the bench areas.

Containers and soil mixes. Clay pots are the best containers, since they are heavy; bromeliads grown in a plastic pot tend to get top-heavy. Because their root systems are so small, a 4- or 5-inch pot will be large enough. Fill the container ⅓ full of pebbles or broken clay pot shards; then add the potting mix. Staking may be necessary until the roots take hold.

Since most bromeliads are epiphytes, they have very small, shallow root systems. They can even be grown on slabs of bark (see photo on page 71, bottom left) or on driftwood. A porous, well-drained soil is best. You can use a commercial

Aechmea chantinii *has olive to brownish green leaves barred with silver. Flower cluster's yellowish blooms have orange, red, or pink bracts tipped yellow and white.*

potting mix or make your own mix: a good one for epiphytic bromeliads is 1 part soil (sterilized), 1 part coarse or sharp river sand, 1 part peat moss, and ½ part crushed granite, fir bark, or osmunda fiber.

Watering and fertilizing. The bromeliads that grow in the vase form need to have their cups filled with water to prevent wilting. To fill the cups, sprinkle with a hose or hand mist sprayer once or twice a week. Water the potting mix thoroughly around the roots when the soil is dry to the touch. Some species—such as guzmanias, nidulariums, and neoregelias—should never be allowed to dry out.

Fertilize bromeliads regularly with a commercial liquid plant food diluted to half the strength recommended by the manufacturer. The cups or vases can be filled occasionally with this diluted fertilizer mixture.

Try these in your greenhouse

Listed in the following paragraphs are those bromeliads that are most commonly grown. Except where special care is recommended, all of these plants like the general care and environment outlined at left and above. This list includes a wide range of plant types, but there are many more for the avid collector to search out.

Aechmea. These vase-shaped bromeliads need shade. Water them only when potting mix has dried out completely. *A. chantinii* has brownish green leaves barred with silver. The flower cluster is yellow with orange red, red, or pink bracts tipped in yellow and white. *A. fasciata* has green leaves with white bands and a powdery coating. Flowers are blue, changing to deep rose with age. Bracts are pink. *A. fulgens discolor* has green leaves backed with purple. Its red flowers are tipped with blue and are followed by rose-colored berries. *A. penduliflora* has strap-shaped, glossy green leaves that turn to maroon in strong light. Clusters of yellow flowers grow on tall stems above red bracts. The hybrid *A.* 'Red Wine' has dark green leaves backed in a wine color. Deep orange flowers are tipped with blue.

Billbergia nutans. This bromeliad grows in the rosette form. It has green leaves with a silver cast underneath. Chartreuse flowers on long stems are tipped in violet blue; bracts are pink. The flowers grow in clusters, and blossoms open one by one for a long-lasting display. Billbergia can be grown as a terrestrial.

Cryptanthus zonatus 'Zebrinus'. Stiff, reddish bronze leaves with silver bands characterize this terrestrial plant. The white flowers grow in a cluster.

Dyckia fosteriana. This terrestrial bromeliad has silvery gray leaves and orange flowers on a tall stem. It likes full sun.

Guzmania lingulata. Rosettes of smooth, metallic green leaves are centered with red bracts; the inner bracts are orange red tipped with white or yellow. The white flowers are insignificant. Direct sunlight can burn the foliage.

Neoregelia carolinae 'Tricolor'. The leaves of this bromeliad are green and white striped, turning pink near the center of the plant. Blue flowers are formed in the cup at the center of the rosette.

Nidularium innocentii. The straplike leaves of this plant have spiny margins. Bases of leaves are brilliant red, giving the rosette a red heart. White flowers with erect petals grow in a dense cluster.

Tillandsia ionantha. This plant grows to only 4 inches in height. Leaves in the center of the plant turn bright red just preceding the appearance of the violet flower clusters. Tillandsia grows best on a branch or piece of bark.

Vriesia 'Mariae'. Yellow flowers rise above light green leaves. The bracts are red at the base, yellow dotted with brown at the tip. *V. splendens* 'Major' has dark green leaves banded with reddish purple. The tall, long-lasting, flattened flower spike has yellowish white flowers sheathed in red bracts.

Cryptanthus zonatus 'Zebrinus' *has stiff, reddish bronze leaves with wavy silver crossbands. New leaves emerge from "vase" or center of plant. Bromeliads like the vase kept filled with water.*

Tillandsia ionantha *is a tiny bromeliad that grows up to 4 inches high. Tufts have thick and narrow leaves covered with silvery bristles.*

Vriesia 'Mariae' *has light green leaves with flattened clusters of yellow flowers. Blooms are encased in bracts that are red at the base, yellow dotted brown at the tip.*

The dramatic duo: cactus and succulents

Many plant collectors who specialize in growing cactus and succulents prefer to keep them in greenhouses. Why, you ask? We all know that cactus and succulents are generally desert plants that don't need the high humidity and stable temperatures of a greenhouse environment. But they all need to be protected from the danger of frost. As all collectors know, one plant leads to a hundred, so a greenhouse offers a very practical way to care for large numbers of similar plants. And, inside the greenhouse, these plants will bloom.

The cactus and succulent plant families are usually discussed together, because their growth needs are so similar. The plants themselves have a lot in common, too. Succulents, strictly speaking, include any plant that stores water in juicy leaves, stems, or roots to withstand periodic drought. True succulent collectors exclude epiphytic orchids and bromeliads and may include some nonfleshy desert plants such as yuccas and puyas. Most succulents are native to desert or semidesert areas in the warmer regions of the world, notably Mexico and South Africa. A few are from colder climates. While it's true that these plants can survive extended droughts, they usually drop leaves, shrivel, or lose leaf color.

Cactus are also succulents. They are generally leafless with modified stems shaped like cylinders, pads, or joints that can store water in anticipation of future droughts. Their thick skins reduce evaporation, and most species have spines for protection. Flowers are usually large and brightly colored. All (with the inevitable one possible exception) are native to the Americas. Many are native to the arid regions, but some grow high in the mountains or in dripping jungles. Cactus plants range in height from a few inches to 50 feet.

Greenhouse "naturals"

The five main reasons cactus and succulents grow well in the greenhouse are protection from frost, protection from the hot sun, good ventilation, lots of heat, and the optimum amount of light. A clear or white roof of rigid plastic offers bright light with no burning sunlight. Shading can also serve as a protection from scorching light for tender varieties (see pages 38-39 for further information) .

Removable wall panels *are covered with polyethylene plastic; can be removed occasionally to increase fresh air ventilation— important for succulents and cactus.*

One cactus and succulent collector feels a round or dome-shaped greenhouse is best for utilizing all possible sunlight. A round shape also gives more bench space than other greenhouse shapes, a real plus if your plant collection is large.

And they can take it

Part of the charm of these plant families is their lack of demands. These plants can survive even the worst conditions. If you cater to their preferences, though, they will reward you with lush growth and beautiful, if unusual, flowers. Listed in succeeding paragraphs are the general growth requirements for cactus and succulents. These plants comprise such large and diverse families that even a partial listing of plant species would be inadequate. So few are difficult to grow, even the beginner should be successful. A good beginning source book would be the *Sunset* book *Succulents and Cactus.*

Light. The hardier varieties can handle full sun; more tender varieties should be shaded to prevent scorching. You would be wise to familiarize yourself with the specific needs of the various plants you grow, so you can protect any tender plants that tend to sunburn.

Temperature. Most cactus and succulents can take any amount of summer heat, but they need to be protected from frost. Forty degrees is usually considered the minimum temperature for these plants in a greenhouse.

Ventilation. A must for cactus and succulents is ventilation. Circulating fans and automatic vents will be helpful. You can also provide ventilating strips or other openings for hot air to escape through. Another solution is to have wall panels on your greenhouse that can be removed during hot weather months (see photographs at bottom right and on page 72).

Containers and potting mixes. Clay pots are considered best, since most cactus and succulents need to dry out between waterings. Adequate drainage is essential. Plastic pots can be used if you are careful to avoid overwatering.

A good all-purpose potting mix for cactus and succulents is a mixture of 1½ cubic feet of organic matter (leaf mold or peat moss are possibilities), 1½ cubic feet sharp river sand, ¾ pound complete fertilizer (buy a dry fertilizer with 12

percent nitrogen) and 2 pounds limestone. This mix provides you with 3 cubic feet of potting soil. If this is more than you need or have room to store, buy commercially prepared cactus mixes.

Watering and fertilizing. A general rule of thumb is to let the potting mix dry out to a depth of about an inch. To test this, stick your index finger into the soil to between the first and second knuckles. If the soil feels dry, soak it thoroughly and let the excess water drain out. Be careful not to wet the foliage; it may rot.

A good potting mix should provide your plant with its needed nutrients for at least a year. Then, the second year, fertilize with a liquid fertilizer diluted to half the strength recommended by the manufacturer. Do this about once a month during the growing season.

Center roof opening *of circular greenhouse allows for fresh air ventilation; plastic dome covers it during periods of inclement weather. Glass roof, walls admit maximum light.*

Scrap lumber benches *rest on concrete blocks (left). Corrugated fiberglass roof protects plants from sunburn.* **Right:** *Wall panels of flat fiberglass hang from hooks on side of greenhouse, are easily removed for ventilation.*

African violets and their relatives

Next to orchids, African violets are the most frequently grown greenhouse plants—as house plants, they probably rank number one. In the greenhouse, African violets receive optimum light and humidity levels that promote lush foliage and abundant flowers. Less perfect conditions usually yield the all-too-familiar poorly shaped plants that can seldom be coaxed into bloom.

African violets (their true botanical genus name is *Saintpaulia*) are members of a large plant family called gesneriads. Many of their relatives, listed on the next page, also make good greenhouse plants.

They like tender, loving care

Though most gardeners can succeed in growing African violets, understanding and meeting their cultural guidelines will promote the best possible performance. These guidelines follow. Do keep in mind that different varieties react to the same growing conditions in different ways. Some African violets will be profuse bloomers; other plants may be stingy with their flowers. If masses of flowers are your goal, you will probably be happier if you replace the shy bloomers with proven plants.

Light. African violets will use all the light they can get. They like some sun but must be shaded from full summer sun; otherwise the foliage may burn. If the foliage turns yellow and has burned edges, the plant has had too much sun. Too little light causes the plants to grow dark green foliage and produce few flowers. Modified light coming through rigid plastic roof and wall coverings in the greenhouse is ideal.

Temperature. A warm greenhouse environment is the African violet's choice. A daytime temperature range of 72° to 75° with a drop to the 60s during the night is good. Some temperature variation is essential for healthy plants. Temperatures over 75° may harm these plants, so move them to the coolest portion of your greenhouse on very hot days. The minimum temperature level is 55°.

Ventilation. Good air circulation is vital to healthy African violets. There should be no direct drafts, though. Be sure your ventilating fans are not aimed directly at the benches. Don't crowd your plants together; give each specimen breathing room. A good idea is to have slots or regularly spaced openings in the greenhouse benches.

Containers and potting mix. You can grow African violets in any kind of pot, but clay pots are preferred by most specialists. They are porous and will not hold moisture; excess salts from too much fertilizer may also filter out, helping prevent fertilizer burn. Containers must have adequate drainage holes and smooth rims.

Several packaged African violet potting mixes are commercially available. These are probably the best bet.

African violet, *a multicrown plant, produces over 100 pink flowers. This plant is called 'Rhapsodie Gisela'. Perfectly round shape is achieved by rotating plant toward light.*

Specially formulated for growing these plants, they are easy to use and store.

Watering and fertilizing. African violets can be watered from the top or the bottom, whichever method you find easier. The water itself should always be at room temperature; cold water on the leaves can cause spotting. To water from the bottom, put water in the saucer and let the soil soak it up by capillary action. For top watering, soak the potting mix completely and then let the excess drain away. Again, avoid getting the foliage wet; you could cause leaf spotting or crown rot. Keep the potting mix evenly moist but not soggy.

You can buy commercially prepared African violet fertilizer. This is probably best for the novice; be sure to follow carefully the directions on the label. To be on the safe side, use a little less fertilizer than recommended.

Meet the relatives

These cousins of the African violet are also interesting plants in the greenhouse, and the plant collector will probably want to try all of them. Generally they prefer the same growing conditions as the African violet; any differences are stated.

Three-tiered cart *holds collection of African violets. Artificial light helps to keep plants symmetrical, promotes blooms. Light units are made of redwood 1 by 4s with 4-foot-long fluorescent fixtures.*

Achimenes. There are many hybrids of this gesneriad. Plants have tubular flowers in white, pink, blue, purple, red, orange, and yellow. Foliage—roundish or oval in bright to dark green—forms either upright or spreading growth. You will need to start these plants from rhizomes (creeping stems) sold by specialty mail-order suppliers; they are rarely sold as growing plants. These plants go dormant in the fall and lose their leaves. You can leave the rhizome in the pot without water or store it until spring.

Aeschynanthus. Sometimes called *Trichosporum*, these species are native to Southeast Asia. Their trailing growth is best in hanging baskets. They need higher temperatures and humidity and more light than most gesneriads.

Columnea. These plants are native to tropical America. Most have a trailing growth habit and can be used in hanging baskets. Columneas have attractive foliage and brilliant flowers, usually in reds and oranges. Epiphytic plants, they will do well if you add some sand or perlite to African violet soil mix for their potting soil. They prefer slightly cool temperatures (about 55° to 60°).

Episcia. A requirement for these plants is a greenhouse with daytime temperatures around 75° and no lower than 60° at night. They like more water and higher humidity than African violets. Their foliage is often colorful and variegated. Tubular flowers come in red, pink, orange, yellow, white, lavender, and spotted combinations of two colors. Episcias grow like strawberries, spreading by runners that produce tiny new plants at the ends.

Kohleria. The foliage, stems, and even flowers of these plants are covered with a fine fuzz. Flowers are tubular in red, pink, and white; some have purple dots. Kohlerias can be grown as hanging plants or staked to grow upright. They have a dormant period; handle them like achimenes.

Sinningia. Better known as gloxinia, these plants are almost as popular as African violets. Their leaves are similar but much larger. The flowers are large, wide, bell-shaped tubes in white, lavender, pink, red, purple, dark maroon, and various combinations of these colors. These plants grow from tubers and have a dormant season. Gloxinias like warm nighttime temperatures (around 65°) and about 50 percent humidity.

Smithiantha. The species are native to the mountains of Mexico and Guatemala, where they receive cool temperatures and moderate to high humidity. Grow them like achimenes. Smithiantha grows from large rhizomes; plant one to a pot. Their nickname is "temple bells," after their colorful, bell-shaped flowers.

Episcia cupreata, *an African violet relative, has many varieties. Plant has trailing growth habit, grows best in hanging baskets. Like strawberries, episcias form new plantlets at ends of runners.*

Who says bulbs can't be hurried?

Two dozen *double-tipped daffodil bulbs planted closely in wooden container yield showy effect.*

Tulip bulbs *are crowded into round clay pots for profusion of bloom; grouping several pots together gives best display.*

"Forcing" bulbs means that you coax them into blooming weeks or months earlier than they would bloom naturally. By giving them a warm temperature earlier than nature would provide it, you can persuade bulbs to give you a taste of spring when it's still cold and bleak outdoors.

Bulbs and their associates—corms and tubers—contain tiny, dormant plants surrounded by enough nutriment to sustain them through the early stages of growth. The stored food supports the embryo plant until it has formed roots.

A bulb is an underground stem surrounded by thick, overlapping scales that contain food produced by the previous year's growth. In contrast to the pear shape of most bulbs, a corm is usually flat at both the top and bottom. Actually the underground base of the previous year's flower stem, the corm is inflated like two solid lungs, one on each side of the stem's base. A tuber is a swollen, underground stem that may be flattened, rounded, or irregularly shaped. It's often difficult to distinguish between a corm and a tuber. The illustration on the facing page compares all three.

Regardless of where you shop for bulbs, buy the best ones you can find. They are worth the extra expense because of the superior bloom they produce. It's better to get a few good bulbs than many mediocre ones. If you order your bulbs from a catalogue, be sure to do it early, for requests are usually filled in the order in which they're received. When nursery shopping pick the largest, plumpest bulbs available. Check to see that the outer skin hasn't been rubbed off by rough handling; feel the bulbs for softness, which could indicate bruises or rot; and examine the entire bulb for insects. The basal plate (see illustration on facing page) should be undamaged, too, as this is where the roots form. If you can't plant them immediately, store your new bulbs in the dark—light signals the tops to start growing.

Once you have purchased the bulbs, you can begin forcing them, following the five major steps to successful forcing: 1) potting, 2) watering, 3) storing while the roots form, 4) bringing them into the greenhouse, 5) increasing the temperature. If your bulbs weren't precooled (chilled by the grower or nurseryman prior to sale—ask if they were) and if you live in a mild climate you might choose to refrigerate them yourself for the better blooming that results. A stay of four to six weeks in the vegetable crisper provides the cool period needed by certain true bulbs (see chart at right) before they can be successfully forced.

Bulbs can be forced in almost any type of container, though conventional pots are the most successful for large displays of color. Pots having a depth at least twice the bulb's width provide enough soil area for the roots to anchor themselves firmly. Any good potting soil or a soil mix of 2 parts garden loam, 1 part clean sharp sand, and 1 part peat moss will provide a suitable growing medium. Powdered bone meal mixed into the soil is beneficial to the developing roots and flower.

Plant tulips and narcissus with their bulb tips barely protruding from the soil. Hyacinths' tips should be set $\frac{1}{2}$ inch below the soil surface. Plant only one variety to a pot; otherwise, growth and flowering won't be uniform. Plant small bulbs as thickly as possible in a proportionately smaller pot—nothing looks more lost than a few tiny bulb plants scattered about in a large pot. Finally, label all pots to avoid confusion later.

After you've planted the bulbs, soak the containers

in water. Soaking is more efficient than overhead watering, which often doesn't penetrate evenly or sufficiently and can wash out newly inserted soil. Failure to soak bulb pots thoroughly is usually the cause of uneven growth and bloom. Keep the pots watered as necessary throughout the forcing period.

In the next step—storing the pots in a cool, dark place (about 50°)—your aim is to get the strongest possible root growth before the leaves start to lengthen. If top growth begins ahead of root development the buds may never emerge. Bulbs that are grown slowly will develop stronger, longer-lasting blossoms. During the rooting period, which lasts from 8 to 12 weeks, the pots can be stored in a trench under sand or straw, in a dark garage or shed, in a coldframe, under boxes outdoors, or any place where they can be kept cool and in the dark.

After at least 2 months, when you can see roots in the containers' drainage holes, start taking the pots out of storage a few at a time for a succession of bloom. At this point you begin the actual forcing process by introducing the bulbs to warmth and light. Keep the pots out of direct light at about 50° for 2 weeks.

Next, put the pots where the temperature is about 55° or 60°—in the greenhouse, if you keep it within this range, or wherever the temperature is right. The temperature should be raised gradually so the foliage and stems develop before the blooms are forced. After another week or so put the pots in full sunlight, in the greenhouse, being sure to keep them well watered until the blooms open. This is a good time to take them into your living room to enjoy.

You can have daffodils in bloom at Christmas if you plant precooled bulbs in late September. Follow the procedure just outlined, keeping the pots in cool storage (50°) until December 1. At this time put them in the greenhouse or someplace where the temperature is 60°. Flowers should emerge by December 25.

After the blooming period, don't cut off the foliage; it must be left on the plants to feed the bulbs for future bloom. Once a bulb has been forced it can't be forced again satisfactorily. Either discard forced bulbs or plant them in your garden, where they will probably flower their second year out.

The following chart lists some bulbs that grow well in the greenhouse. The true bulbs should be precooled if they are forced in a warm climate or out of season. For more information on the plants listed, refer to the *Sunset* book *How to Grow Bulbs*.

Key: B=bulb; C=corm; T=tuber
c=cool (45-55°) ; m=medium (55-65°) ; w=warm (65-75°)

Plant	Type	When to plant	Expected to bloom	Hardy or tender	Best nighttime temperature
Acidanthera	C	Winter-spring	Spring-summer	t	m
Amarcrinum	B	March	Winter-early spring	t	m
Amaryllis belladonna	B	Fall	Summer	h	c
Anemone	T	September-October	January-March	h	c
Begonia (summer flowering)	T	March	Early summer	t	m
Begonia (hanging)	T	January	June-Fall	t	m
Begonia (winter flowering)	T	Fall	November-March	t	m
Chionodoxa	B	September-October	January-March	h	c
Colchicum	C	August-September	October-December	h	c
Crinum	B	Fall, spring	Summer	t	m
Crocus	C	August-October	December-March	h	c
Cyclamen	T	August	November	h	c
Dahlia	T	February	Summer	t	c-w
Eucomis	B	Fall	Summer	h	c-m
Freesia	C	August-November	December-March	t	c
Galanthus	B	September-October	January-March	h	c
Gladiolus	C	November	February	t	c-m
Haemanthus	B	Winter	Late spring	t	c-m
Hippeastrum	B	October	February-March	t	m
Hyacinth	B	August-September	December-March	h	c
Hymenocallis	B	Spring	Early summer	t	m
Iris	R	September-October	December-April	h	m
Ixia	C	Fall	May-June	t	m
Lachenalia	B	August-September	December	t	c
Lilium	B	Spring, fall	Winter-summer	h	m
Muscari	B	September-October	March-April	h	c
Narcissus	B	August-October	January-April	h	c
Ornithogalum	B	September-October	January-March	h, t	m
Polianthes	T	January-May	June-September	t	m
Scilla	B	September-October	December-March	h	c
Sinningia	T	Any time	Off and on	t	m-w
Tritonia	C	October	April	t	c
Tulipa	B	September-October	December-March	h	c
Vallota	B	July-August	Spring-summer	t	m
Veltheimia	B	August-September	December-April	t	c

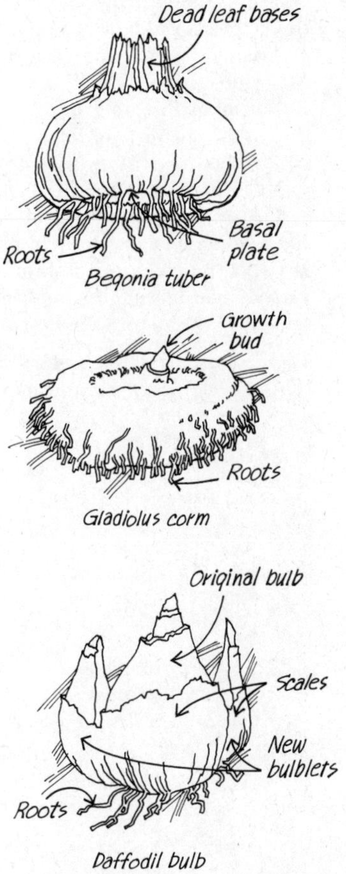

Dead leaf bases

Roots

Basal plate

Begonia tuber

Growth bud

Roots

Gladiolus corm

Original bulb

Scales

New bulblets

Roots

Daffodil bulb

Parts of tuber, *corm, and bulb are detailed above.*

Ferns have a quiet grace

Like cactus and succulents, many ferns are commonly grown in the garden or, like African violets, as house plants. Ferns are such versatile plants that gardeners put them to many uses; their various green tones make them very useful in the landscape or as a special accent indoors. Ferns have a quiet grace and come in a variety of pleasing shapes. But by grouping them all together inside a greenhouse, you will have the advantages of easily catering to their needs and providing the growing space a large plant collection requires.

Ferns are one of the oldest plant forms on our planet and one of the largest families. They produce no flowers, reproducing by spores that form directly on the fronds (leaves). Native varieties hail from all corners of the world; most grow in forests, though some varieties come from tropical jungles, desert areas, open fields, or near the timberline in high mountains. There are spectacular tree ferns with finely cut fronds atop a treelike stem. And there are tiny woodland ferns that serve as ground covers or grow out of crevices in rocks. The peculiar platyceriums (staghorn ferns) have huge fronds shaped like antlers.

Taming the fickle fern

Gardeners have grown ferns ever since that plant's heyday in Victorian England. In fact, "fern house" was a common nickname for the conservatories and greenhouses of that era. Many people consider ferns to be petulant and difficult, if not impossible, to grow. This poor press is probably due to the inability of ferns to adapt to hot, dry growing conditions. Watching them grow in a greenhouse environment is a refreshing experience.

The growing requirements that follow are general guidelines. Some fern species will need different treatment. It's always a good idea to familiarize yourself with the various plants you grow and the culture they require, giving you—and the plant—the best chance for success.

Light. Most ferns like to be shaded from hot, direct sunlight. Though many types can tolerate very low light levels,
it's best to give ferns good, strong, indirect light for the best foliage color.

Inside the greenhouse, provide them with enough shade to prevent them from burning. The north side of your greenhouse would be an ideal location for your fern collection, or you could grow them under the benches. Some gardeners use a layer of shade cloth over the fern benches (see photo on page 39).

Temperature. Ferns should do well in a cool greenhouse. They like temperature levels between 65° and 70° during the day with about a 10° drop at night.

Humidity. In contrast with many tropical plants that like high humidity coupled with warm temperatures, ferns prefer their high humidity in a cool climate. Provide these plants with a minimum of 50 percent humidity; some varieties may want even more.

Ventilation. Ferns, like all the specialty plants we've discussed, need very good air circulation with no direct drafts. Arrange the air movement so that air doesn't blow directly onto the plant benches. Also, ferns do best on benches with slots or regularly spaced openings that allow air to circulate freely around the pots.

Ferns hate to be crowded together. They like to unfurl their fronds in lots of open space. Many ferns, especially those with trailing fronds, grow best when put in hanging baskets or on pedestals.

Containers and potting mix. Ferns seem to be partial to clay pots, though any other type of container should work as well. The advantage of clay is that it's porous, allowing excess moisture and harmful salts to filter out the sides. Hanging ferns can be potted in wire baskets lined with sphagnum moss. Some of the epiphytic ferns (those that grow on trees in the wild and depend on the air and rain to provide them with water and nutrients) like to grow on moss-covered wooden slabs or pieces of tree bark just as they would in nature; this is pictured on the next page.

Use a potting mix that is porous and retains moisture, yet lets any excess water drain away rapidly. Ferns need

Nephrolepis exaltata 'Smithii' has lacy, almost feathery fronds; grows best in hanging baskets or on pedestals so fronds can hang down. This fern can grow in a shade or lath house in mild climates.

Platycerium ferns *grow mounted on wooden slabs. Roots are protected by roundish frond called a shield. Antlerlike fronds inspire plant's nickname, "staghorn fern."*

to have air circulating freely around their roots. There are many commercial mixes you can buy that will work well. To make the mix spongier, you can add chopped sphagnum or leaf mold.

Watering and fertilizing. True moisture lovers, ferns should never be allowed to dry out. Keep their potting mix constantly moist but never let it get waterlogged. Ferns growing in hanging baskets or on slabs or bark will dry out more rapidly than those in other containers. Watch these plants carefully.

If you fertilize your ferns, use a water soluble commercial fertilizer that is high in nitrogen. The best way to use fertilizer is to dilute it to half the recommended strength and apply it half as often as the label states. Some gardeners, though, find that ferns dislike being fertilized—it causes leaves to burn or dry up.

Unique problems. Ferns are less susceptible to insect and pest attacks than most other greenhouse plants. Unfortunately, if they do become infested, they react so badly to most pesticides that you may lose them anyway. Your best remedy for a pest problem is to wash the plants off frequently with a forceful spray of water, in a sink, bathtub, or outdoors with a hose. Snails and slugs rank fern fronds among great delicacies, so put out lots of bait.

Your choice is broad

The following list describes some of the more commonly grown ferns. Most of them prefer the climate found in a cool greenhouse; any differences in growing requirements will be stated in the individual plant listing.

Adiantum. Called maidenhair fern because of their delicately cut fronds, these plants are mostly native to the tropics. A few come from temperate North America. They will respond well to the general growing requirements given for ferns. Be sure that their potting mix is rich in organic matter; add enough leaf mold, peat moss, or chopped sphagnum moss to make the potting mix spongy.

Asplenium. Two main types of this fern are commonly grown. *A. bulbiferum* is called the mother fern because new, tiny plantlets are formed on its fronds. This fern is native to Malaysia and New Zealand. *A. nidus* has long, uncut

fronds—apple green with a black rib—that unfurl from the plant center. Be careful when watering; water accumulation in the crown may cause the plant to rot. Fronds dislike being touched.

Cibotium glaucum. This tree fern from Hawaii has feathery golden green fronds. It likes warmer temperatures than most ferns, so place it in a warm corner of a cool greenhouse or grow it in a warm greenhouse.

Cyrtomium falcatum. Native to Japan, this plant is nicknamed the holly fern because its dark green, leathery, glossy fronds are toothed like Christmas holly. It can stand lower humidity levels than most ferns. Be careful not to bury the upper surface of the root ball when repotting.

Davallia. This group of ferns is characterized by brownish, furry, creeping stems—called rhizomes—that grow above the soil. The various nicknames refer to the rhizomes' resemblance to animals' feet. These plants are well suited to hanging baskets. *D. fijiensis* is called the rabbit's foot fern. It has brown, woolly, creeping stems. *D. trichomanoides,* the squirrel's foot fern, is larger with reddish brown rhizomes.

Humata tyermannii. Called the bear's foot fern because of its furry creeping rhizomes, this small fern is native to China. Fronds are very finely cut. Humata resembles davallia, but it is slower growing.

Lygodium japonicum. Native to southeast Asia, this climbing fern has lacy-textured, light green fronds. The fertile fronds (those that produce spores) are much narrower than the sterile ones. Grow it on a trellis or in a hanging basket.

Nephrolepis. Considered by many gardeners the easiest fern to grow, nephrolepis has many varieties. The fronds are sword-shaped with closely spaced leaflets, some more finely cut than others. These ferns look spectacular displayed on pedestals. *N. exaltata* 'Bostoniense,' the Boston fern, is probably the most popular indoor fern.

Pellaea. These small ferns have detailed fronds. *P. rotundifolia* is called the button fern because its dark green leaflets are almost round. *P. viridis* has fronds that vary from oval to lance-shaped on the same plant.

Phyllitis scolopendrium. From Europe and the eastern United States, this unusual fern has glossy, undivided, strap-shaped fronds. Its nickname, hart's tongue fern, comes from the shape of the frond.

Placyterium. Called the staghorn fern because its fronds resemble antlers, this plant is native to the tropics. In nature these ferns grow on trees; most gardeners grow them on slabs of bark or on pieces of tree fern stem. They have two kinds of fronds—sterile ones (no spores) that are flat and pale green aging to tan, and fertile fronds that are forked. They can be grown in a cool greenhouse or in a shade or lath house.

Polypodium aureum. This fern is native to tropical America. Its heavy, brown, hairy creeping rhizomes account for its nickname, the hare's foot fern. It likes a potting mix that is high in organic matter.

Pteris. These tiny, delicate ferns are best known for their forked and crested, plain or variegated fronds. They are native to the tropics.

Pyrrosia lingua. Sometimes sold as *Cyclophorus lingua,* this fern from Japan has dark green, broad, undivided, lance-shaped fronds with a feltlike texture and creeping rootstocks. This slow-growing plant is most often grown in hanging baskets.

A timetable for flowering plants

Like lights in a cave, gaily colored flowers can brighten your greenhouse on dismal winter days—or on any day, for that matter. And you can have flowers in bloom throughout the year in your greenhouse with little effort.

Nurturing a dustlike seed into a bushy plant and finally getting it to reward you with a splash of color is one of the greatest pleasures gardening offers. Flowering time is determined by the date you start your plants—and there's leeway here, for you can start many plants almost any time during the year. Good gardening practices such as tip pinching and applying bottom heat can influence flowering, too.

You can really startle your friends with out-of-season blooms. Do you need a centerpiece for your Christmas dinner table? Try a bouquet of red snapdragons and white asters. A January retirement party for your boss? Arrange some anthurium blooms and osmanthus leaves. Having a tea for the PTA on Washington's birthday?

Give red ranunculus, white stock, and blue pansies the spotlight.

Your greenhouse is the key to getting flowers to bloom when they normally wouldn't. You can control temperature and humidity accurately enough to imitate the different seasons. Experiment a little and you'll probably be surprised by an array of color.

The following two charts exemplify plants that bloom well in the greenhouse. The first chart lists plants you can get to bloom in the greenhouse at almost any time of year; the other one lists plants that will bloom in the greenhouse but might not survive a winter outside, except in very warm areas. Propagation times in the greenhouse may differ from when you would normally plant outside.

Use the "Propagation Key" to help you decide on the best way to start your plants. The "Temperature Key" points out the most desirable nighttime temperatures for the different plants.

Propagation key: C=cutting; D=division; L=leaf; R=rhizome; S=seed

Temperature key: c=cool (45-55°) ; m=medium (55-65°) ; w=warm (65-75°)

Plant	How to propagate	When to propagate	Expected to bloom	Best nighttime temperature
Abutilon	S, C	Spring, summer	Late fall	c
Ageratum	S	February-March	Late spring	c
Anthurium	S, D	Any time	Almost continuously	w
Begonia (fibrous)	S	June	December	m-w
Browallia	S	February	Spring	c-m
Calendula	S	Late July	January	c
Callistephus	S	Fall-winter	Winter-spring	m
Gypsophila	S	December	March	c
Impatiens	S, C	August	Winter	m
Lantana	S	Spring	Almost continuously	c-m
Lathyrus	S	September-October	December-May	c
Lobelia erinus	S	Any time	All year	c
Lobularia	S	Any time	All year	c
Myosotis	S, C	June-August	Winter	c
Nemesia	S	August	October-February	c
Pelargonium	C	Summer	Almost continuously	c
Salpiglossis	S	Fall-winter	Winter-spring	c-m
Tagetes	S	Fall	Winter	m
Trachymene	S	June-August	December-February	c
Tropaeolum	S	Any time	Almost continuously	c
Tulbaghia fragrans	S	Any time	Almost continuously	c
Zantedeschia	R	Late summer	Almost any time	m
Zinnia	S	Fall-winter	Winter-spring	m

Plant	How to propagate	When to propagate	Expected to bloom	Best nighttime temperature
Acalypha hispida	C	Any time	Varies, October-April	m
Achimenes	R, C	Spring	Summer	m
Aeschynanthus	S, L, C	Spring	Summer	m
Allamanda	C	February-April	June-September	w
Alstroemeria	S	August	March-July	m
	D	Spring	March-July	m
Antirrhinum	S	Any time	All year	c
Azalea	C	May	Winter-spring	c-m
Begonia (Rhizomatous)	R	Spring	Summer	m-w
	C	Any time	Almost continuously	m-w
Beloperone	C	Summer	All year	c
Bougainvillea	C	Summer	Almost continuously	m
Browallia	S	July-August	Winter	c-m
Brunfelsia	C	Spring	January-September	c
Calceolaria	S	August-September	March	c
Camellia	C	Fall	Spring	c
Campanula	S	Spring	Late spring-fall	c
	C	Summer	Late spring-fall	c
Cattleya	D	Spring	Summer	m
Chrysanthemum	C	April-June	October-December	c
Clerodendrum	S, C	January	April-September	m-w
Cymbidium	D	Spring	Winter-summer	c
Delphinium	S	Late summer	Spring-summer	c-m
Dianthus	C	December	Summer-fall	c
Epidendrum	D	Early spring	Spring	m
Euphorbia pulcherrima	C	May-August	Winter	m
Euphorbia milii	C	Summer	Almost continuously	m
Felicia	S	September	March	c
Fuchsia	C	October-March	Summer-fall	c
Gardenia	C	December-March	Spring-summer	w
Heliotropium	S	Spring	Spring-summer	m
	C	Summer	Spring-summer	m
Kalanchoe	S	March	December	c-w
Lycaste	D	Spring	Winter	c
Matthiola	S	August-February	January-June	c
Miltonia	D	Spring	Summer-fall	m
Odontoglossum	D	Spring, fall	Spring-fall	c
Oncidium	D	Spring	Spring-summer	c
Osmanthus	C	June	Spring	c
Paphiopedilum	D	After bloom	Winter or summer	c-m
Passiflora	S, C	Spring	Summer	m
Phalaenopsis	S	After bloom	Spring	m-w
Plumbago	C	Summer	Spring-fall	c
Primula	S	April-July	January-May	c
Ranunculus	S	Fall-spring	January-March	c
Rosa	C	Spring	Spring-summer	c-m
Saintpaulia	S, L	Any time	Any time	w
Schizanthus	S	August	March-April	c
Senecio	S	June-September	January-May	c
Streptocarpus	S	Spring-fall	Fall-winter	w
Streptosolen	C	Summer	April-October	m
Trachelospermum	C	Summer	Spring-fall	c
Viola	S	Fall-winter	Winter-spring	c
Zygocactus	C	September	December	m

Gardening in a controlled environment

Plants, like people, prefer certain living conditions, and they perform best when these special needs are catered to. The best way you can handle plants that won't grow naturally in your climate is to provide them with a greenhouse environment controlled to their liking.

Greenhouses are usually controlled within specific temperature levels: the cool greenhouse maintains a nighttime temperature range of 45° to 55°; a warm greenhouse, on the other hand, is kept from 55° to 70° during the night. Of course these temperature ranges will overlap somewhat, and each type of greenhouse has some warm or cold areas that will allow you to grow a few plants outside the temperature range you normally provide. A combination greenhouse incorporating both a cool and a warm chamber is the most versatile of all.

On the following pages we present many of the different kinds of gardening and the variety of plants you can grow in each of these specially controlled greenhouses. The shade or lath house and the garden room, which also provide you with specialized growing areas, are also discussed.

If your greenhouse is cool . . .

The cool greenhouse attempts to maintain its environment at a nighttime temperature of 40° to 55° and a daytime high of around 70° to 75°. Humidity levels will depend on the specific plants you select—most cactus and succulents, for example, thrive in relatively low humidity; ferns tend to like higher levels; both need a cool greenhouse.

This kind of greenhouse climate caters to plants that in nature prefer cooler temperatures but still need protection from frost. These plants would come from moderate climate areas within the temperate zones, most woodland areas, or high altitude areas in tropical regions.

Temperature control

Maintaining the environment inside the cool greenhouse will require a heating system (pages 30-31), a ventilating system (pages 33-34), and a cooling system (page 34). Equipment for providing humidity (page 34) is optional. Most cool-temperature greenhouses also need shading during the hot weather months; see pages 38-39 for ways to shade.

On the average, a cool greenhouse will be less expensive to operate than a warm greenhouse. The heating system, especially in milder climate areas, may not be needed on a day-to-day basis. Usually, operating it a few hours during the night will be all that's required. In a harsh climate, the heating system will receive more use, but it will still be less expensive than operating a greenhouse to maintain the warm temperature ranges.

Cooling will be a necessity. An adequate cooling system will prevent the temperature from rising too much above the maximum levels most of your plants prefer. Even during the winter months, natural solar heat can raise the greenhouse interior above the 75° level. If you live in a warm climate, adequate cooling systems will be even more critical. Keeping your cool greenhouse cool will be an added expense.

Ideas for year-around use

Your cool-temperature greenhouse will keep you busy gardening all year around. Each season offers new challenges,

Rhododendrons grown from seed *were started inside a cool greenhouse—temperatures 55° to 65°. Flats containing potted seedlings have heating coils under soil to keep soil temperature at 72°. When seedlings are 2 years old, they go into garden.*

and you can have the satisfaction of completing one project and turning to another. You can also grow specialty plants—some family groups prefer the cool greenhouse, while certain members of other large plant families also need the lower temperatures.

The following paragraphs cover the ways a cool greenhouse is most frequently put to use.

Wintering tender plants. Many plants we grow in containers during the summer can be carried over through the winter for use in subsequent seasons. The only problem is that many of these plants aren't frost hardy. But by storing them in your greenhouse, you can bring them back to grow another year.

Two popular plants react well to this treatment: fuchsias and geraniums. Before the first frost hits, make room in your greenhouse. If your greenhouse has glass-to-ground construction, you can store them under the benches (be sure they are protected from any drips or runoff caused by watering). Otherwise, make room for them on an empty bench. Since they won't need much care, they can be placed in those awkward corners that are hard to reach. Both plants will need severe pruning; save the trimmings to start

Cymbidium collection *thrives in greenhouse having lath sides, corrugated plastic roof. To set flower buds, cool nighttime temperatures of 45° to 55° are a must. 12-inch opening at top of walls help to keep temperatures constant.*

Cuttings *are placed in box containing vermiculite rooting mix heated to 70° by a heating cable placed in the bottom of box. Camellia, geranium cuttings are being started.*

new plants. Both hardwood and softwood cuttings are discussed on pages 58-59.

If you have other perennial plants that can't take the winter in your climate, try carrying them over, too.

Starting seeds and cuttings. Another way your cool greenhouse helps you get a head start on your spring and summer gardening is by starting seeds and cuttings. You can buy seeds as soon as they're available in garden centers or through seed catalogues. Try to start them a month to 6 weeks before you'd normally plant them in the ground. You'll have well-established seedlings to put out once the frost danger is past. Another advantage of growing plants from seed is that you can get exactly the plants you want. People without a greenhouse (or a coldframe; see pages 42-43) have to settle for the plants or seeds they can find in commercial outlets.

Many seeds require bottom heating or a warmer temperature than that in your cool greenhouse. You can still accommodate these plants by using a seed flat with heating coils (see page 43).

Growing plants from cuttings allows you to start more plants of a specimen you particularly like for its foliage or flowers. And most cuttings cost you nothing. As a group, gardeners are probably the friendliest people you'll find; they're always willing to share cuttings from favorite plants. For more information on rooting cuttings, see pages 58-59.

Raising vegetables. Home vegetable gardens are cropping up everywhere, and a greenhouse can be invaluable as a source of seedlings. You can also grow cool season vegetables, both spring and fall, right inside the greenhouse. Such vegetables as lettuce, endive, green onions, spinach, and turnips can be grown in beds or large flats. If you have lots of room, consider growing broccoli, Brussels sprouts, cauliflower, celery, and peas. Raising food crops in your greenhouse is discussed in more detail on pages 60-61.

Early bloomers. Some early blooming plants, like azaleas, camellias, and cyclamen, bloom in late winter or early spring. These plants can grow nicely in mild or moderately cold climates, but in harsh climates they need some protection. A cool greenhouse is the perfect shelter, provided you have enough room. When they're in bloom, bring them out and display them, but remember to return them in the evening.

Both azaleas and camellias need acid soil mixes and acid fertilizers; these are available commercially. Or you can make your own soil mix by adding large quantities of peat moss to regular potting soil. Some azalea growers use straight peat moss as a growing medium. Both azaleas and camellias need fast-draining soils, and both like mulches to keep their root areas moist.

Cyclamen and other bulb or tuber plants are discussed on pages 76-77.

Forcing bulbs. Another way to get early color, both for your house and outdoors, is to force bulbs, such as daffodils and tulips, into early bloom. In many harsh winter areas, bulbs grown in the ground don't emerge until late spring. A flowering daffodil in February, though, can raise the spirits of people who are still snowbound. The method of forcing bulbs into early bloom is described on pages 76-77.

Growing specialty plants. Many specialty plants prefer the environment of a cool greenhouse. Most cactus and succulents (pages 70-71), ferns (pages 78-79), and some orchids (pages 64-69) and bromeliads (pages 70-71) prefer these temperatures. If you want to grow a few of the warmer-blooded plants, find a warm corner, use bottom heating coils in a flat or bench, or try artificial lights.

If your greenhouse is warm...

Similar in environment to steamy tropical jungles filled with exotic plants and beautiful flowers, the warm greenhouse maintains a temperature range between 55° and 70° during the night with daytime levels between 75° and 85°. Most warm greenhouses also maintain humidity levels around 50 percent or higher, depending on the plants.

This controlled climate lets the gardener fill his greenhouse with those unusual plants native to the tropical areas of the world. And many of the plants we grow in our homes as house plants will not only flourish in a warm greenhouse, they may even bloom.

Temperature control

In order to keep the warm greenhouse controlled, you will need a heating system, a ventilating system, a cooling system, and a system for providing humidity. You will also require some form of shading. An alarm system and some automatic controls are recommended, too.

A warm greenhouse demands very specific controls—be prepared for the energy costs involved. All these systems need some form of fuel or energy to operate, and some will be more expensive than others. If you live in a cold winter climate, your heating will be even more costly. Therefore, you'll be wise to find the most efficient heating system you can afford. Heating equipment is discussed in detail on pages 30-31.

The ventilation system will provide your plants with fresh air; it is also helpful in keeping the temperatures cool, since hot air escapes through the vents in the roof and is replaced by cooler air coming in through the floor vents. It's best to have automatic equipment to open these vents, as temperatures can rise rapidly inside a glass house and do much damage before you are aware of it. Some systems can operate without electricity; see pages 33-34 for information.

A cooling system is also a must. Though the plants you will grow in a warm greenhouse like warmish nights, they prefer the daytime temperatures to remain in the 80s. A thermostatically controlled cooling system will prevent your plants from cooking on very hot days. Various methods of cooling a greenhouse are covered on page 34.

Higher humidity levels are needed for many of the plants grown in warm greenhouses. You can help provide humidity manually by such methods as keeping gravel or sawdust under the benches damp or hand misting with a mister or a misting nozzle attached to a hose. The best method of insuring a steady level of humidity in your greenhouse is to install a humidifier operated by a humidistat. Another way would be to attach mist nozzles to a timer. The various methods of maintaining humidity are discussed on page 34.

Because the controlled environment of the warm greenhouse is essential to the well-being of your plants, an alarm system that signals a dangerous situation—either the failure of a system to operate or a power outage—is highly recommended. These systems are discussed on page 35.

Greenhouse for vegetables *is located in Alaska, where tomatoes, cucumbers would never ripen during short summer season. Greenhouse also contains annuals, many tropical plants. In milder climates, a warm greenhouse can produce vegetables out of season.*

Unless you have a great deal of free time throughout each day to devote to running your greenhouse, automating the various systems that control the atmosphere is almost a necessity. Operating each system manually is time consuming, and you must constantly monitor the temperature and humidity levels. Many of the systems come with built-in automation; others can be hooked up to timers. Automating the greenhouse has the added advantage of allowing you to leave on vacations without hiring a full-time keeper.

Ideas for year-round use

A warm greenhouse knows no season—it keeps a consistent temperature and humidity level throughout the year, and you can even control day length by using artificial lights. Here are a few of the common types of gardening you can accomplish within your constant climate.

Growing tropical plants. Probably the most frequent function of a warm greenhouse is growing tropical plants—those that in nature come from the tropical regions of the world. Orchids are perhaps the most familiar and popular plants that fall into this category; the most common orchids are covered on pages 64-69. Other types of plants include bromeliads (pages 70-71), tropical ferns (pages 78-79), and the other interesting vines and plants native to the tropics.

Since interior temperatures fluctuate somewhat, your greenhouse may have some coolish spots where you can grow plants that prefer the cooler weather conditions. It's wise to attempt only those plants that like cool temperatures coupled with higher humidity. Bromeliads (pages 70-71) and some cactus and succulents (pages 72-73) are other possible candidates.

Raising vegetables. Your warm greenhouse is perfect for warm season vegetables. Tomatoes and cucumbers adapt well to cultivation inside a greenhouse. And because of the constant climate, you can enjoy fresh produce the year around, though you may have to pollinate the vegetable plants by hand. Other warm weather crops can also be grown.

Since these vegetables need sunlight for their best performance, you may want to avoid shading the parts of your greenhouse where vegetables are grown. If you plan to grow vegetables only, you won't need an elaborate humidifier. Growing food crops is discussed on pages 60-61.

Plants from seeds and cuttings. Your warm greenhouse, just like the cool greenhouse, can be used to start new plants from seeds or cuttings. Flats equipped with heating coils will get your seedlings off to a good start (see pages 42-43). Cuttings can also be started in flats or containers; the high humidity within the warm greenhouse will help keep the cuttings from wilting or drying out. Starting new plants from cuttings is covered on pages 58-59.

Reviving house plants. Tropical plants that we grow inside our homes suffer from our dry, overheated atmospheres. By giving your house plants a respite inside your warm climate greenhouse, you can revitalize them. The high humidity levels and high light levels are perfect.

A word of warning: a house plant that grows in poor light should not be placed directly in the bright light of a greenhouse. Gradually adapt the house plant to the greenhouse interior by keeping it shaded or under a bench for a week or so until it can handle the higher amounts of light. Some of the common house plants are included in the section on garden rooms; see pages 88-91 for a listing.

Orchids, tropical plants *enjoy warm temperatures and 65 percent humidity in prefab greenhouse. Heater and fan keep temperatures constant during cold, warm seasons.*

Translucent fiberglass *covers roof and walls of greenhouse containing several different types of orchids. Fiberglass modifies light so tender plants won't sunburn.*

Vegetables thrive *inside this glass-walled greenhouse. Cucumber vines are supported on string attached to frame. Onions, beets, green peppers also grow in raised bed.*

The best of both worlds: cool and warm

The combination greenhouse offers the gardener the best of both worlds: a cool greenhouse and a warm greenhouse. When you have both, you can attempt any type of greenhouse gardening you wish.

Usually divided by a glass or plastic partition, a combination greenhouse is one structure divided into two individually controlled chambers. If this is planned for in the beginning, you will need to install only one climate control system (heating, ventilation, cooling, and humidity) to serve both rooms. If you add to—or divide—a greenhouse after construction has been completed, you may need to purchase additional systems to properly control both greenhouses.

The extra cost to build a combination house is practically nil, since you only need to add an extra interior wall. (Of course, your greenhouse will have to be large enough to provide two rooms of reasonable size.) The equipment systems must be large enough to handle both greenhouses, and separate controls and outlets will be needed in each chamber. This will be slightly more expensive.

Operating a combination greenhouse will probably cost more than running a cool greenhouse of the same size, but it should be about the same as operating a comparable warm greenhouse.

A combination house will be more time-consuming to operate than most other greenhouses, since you will be doing a greater variety of gardening chores. Also, because your plants will be more varied, you could have more problems.

Luckily, the other side of the coin is more positive— you will be free to try all kinds of gardening and to experiment with plants from all parts of the world.

Glass wall separates *warmer greenhouse section from cooler area. Orchids, tropical foliage plants are kept in warm section (foreground); cymbidiums, other cool-temperature plants are in back area.*

Glass-and-metal-framed lean-to *is partitioned into two sections—cooler area is used for starting plants from seeds, cuttings; warmer section contains tropical plants. Note that vent over warmer section is open, other closed.*

Front section *of divided orchid greenhouse is kept at 65° to 85° temperature range. Rear section beyond door is kept warmer with humidity as high as 85 percent. Glass-and-wood partition separates the two sections.*

A sun pit solves some cold winter needs

Do you know what a sun pit is? It's like a greenhouse but simpler—it's basically a large hole in the ground with a glass or fiberglass cover over it. This type of subterranean greenhouse isn't for everyone, but if you live where the ground freezes in winter and the growing season is short, a sun pit or grow hole might be a solution to the problem of cold weather in spring and fall.

The principle is straightforward: the translucent or transparent cover traps a maximum amount of solar radiation, the earth and rocks around the sun pit provide insulation, and solar heat is trapped so efficiently that a heater should be unnecessary. In fact, cooling a grow hole can be a problem during warm summer months.

A grow hole could be used for starting seeds, rooting cuttings, storing plants that have finished blooming, forcing bulbs, and other things you'll think of as you use it. Most plants that like cool nighttime temperatures (45° to 55°) will do well in a sun pit. You can set potted plants on the floor or on benches, or you can plant directly in the floor of the grow hole.

For as much solar radiation as possible, locate your sun pit to face south. It can be against a house, on a slope, or in flat ground. Dig the hole deep enough that the tops of your plants will be below the freezing level of the ground. In fact, it will be easier for you to work around your plants if you dig the pit deep enough to stand up in; this will also insure that most of the plants will be below the freezing level. To save yourself some work, do this: as you remove soil from the hole, mound the soil around its edges to raise the walls above ground level. If your sun pit is in level ground, pile more dirt on the north side so the cover will slope toward the south.

If you put up any support beams or retaining walls in your sun pit, you should use preservative-treated redwood, which won't rot. Use redwood for benches, too, if you plan to install them.

Be sure drainage is adequate; otherwise a heavy rain could turn your sun pit into a swamp. If the soil in your area has a high clay content (which retains water) or if you expect drainage to be a problem for other reasons, dig the hole deeper than necessary, put in drainage pipe or tile, and then backfill. If you plan to plant directly in the floor of your sun pit, be generous in adding amendments to the backfill material; subsurface soil is usually infertile.

When you expect a hard freeze, cover the glass or fiberglass roof with an old carpet, blanket, or some other type of insulating material during the night. Be sure to remove the cover during the day to let light in.

In a cold winter area a sun pit can enable you to get a head start on the growing season. If you have the space, give one a try.

Corrugated fiberglass roof *covers 30 by 40-foot "grow hole" or sun pit (below). Vegetables can be grown the year around. Solar energy provides heat.* **Above:** *Diagram shows that sun pit was placed below freezing level.*

What can you grow in a garden room?

The garden room is a special place set aside for plants and people. It's a place for gardeners to enjoy their plants and for other people to admire those plants. Because it's for people as well as plants, the environment is a compromise between a true greenhouse and an ordinary room in any house; both the people and the plants have to make some concessions.

Making the garden room work

Since the garden room is just another room, its temperatures will be similar to those in the rest of your house, around 65° to 75° during the day, with about a 5° to 10° drop at night. Luckily the tropical plants we grow as house plants like this temperature range, too.

As a room for growing plants, it will make generous use of glass—possibly skylights or a glassed ceiling, as well as large window walls. This will permit lots of light to enter, another similarity to the greenhouse environment.

Humidity is the one problem you'll face. Many of the plants we grow as house plants or tropicals prefer high levels of humidity, as high as 50 percent. Obviously, people don't enjoy levels quite this high. You can install a portable humidifier that will keep the room at about 30 to 40 percent, use humidifying trays (metal or plastic trays filled with pebbles that are kept constantly moist) , or you can use a hand mister frequently. The plants themselves will provide some humidity through transpiration. You can take full advantage of this by grouping many plants together.

Decorating and furnishing will have to bow to the room's special function—especially important are materials that

Two-story entry *was designed specifically for growing house plants—both large and small. Tall ceiling permits owner to grow trees. Window wall lets in maximum light; room is painted white to help reflect light. Aggregate floor with drain next to window makes watering chores easy.*

can't be damaged by excessive amounts of light or moisture. A floor of brick, tile, or aggregate is best, since these materials are impervious to water damage.

You will also want some method of circulating air. Provide window vents both near the floor level and near the roof or ceiling. You may want a circulating fan as well to keep the air moving.

Tropical plants for garden rooms

The following paragraphs list just a few of the tropical plants that will grow well in a garden room. Many of them make adequate house plants. But when you place them in a garden room that meets their growth requirements, you'll find them responding as never before. Many of the plants listed in the section on specialty plants (see pages 64-81) can also be grown in garden rooms; check their growth needs to find likely candidates.

Skylight, large windows *provide ample light in high-ceilinged garden room. Plants sit on floor, low benches—even hang from ceiling. Laminated plastic floor is easy to clean, is not damaged by water.*

Former patio *was enclosed with glass and translucent fiberglass walls; beamed ceiling is also covered with fiberglass. Sliding glass doors separate garden room from house. Brick floor, wrought iron furniture add to atmosphere.*

Most of these plants will thrive in commercially packaged potting mixes for indoor plants, with commercial liquid all-purpose fertilizers used according to package directions. Any exceptions will be noted in the individual plant descriptions.

You can also bring plants normally grown in the greenhouse—such as orchids in bloom or bromeliads—into the house or garden room for display purposes. Try to provide them with most of their preferences; a garden room will be the best place outside the greenhouse for their sojourn. Be sure to return them within a reasonable length of time.

Abutilon. Called Chinese lantern because of the shape of the flowers, this plant comes from South America. It needs to be pinched to keep the growth compact and to extend the blooming period. It can be grown upright or be trained in a hanging basket.

Acalypha hispida. The flowers of this plant are long, fuzzy, tassellike, red or purple blooms that inspire its nickname, chenille plant. The leaves are bright green and hairy. It needs lots of pruning to keep its shape. Keep the potting mix constantly moist but not soggy.

Aglaonema. These hardy plants have oblong leathery leaves, either plain green or variegated. Their small, pale green flowers resemble the calla lily bloom. Better not place this plant on a wooden surface—exudation from leaf tips can spot wood.

Alocasia. Native to tropical Asia, this lush plant has leaves that look like elephant ears. Flowers resemble those of the calla. Add some organic matter (leaf mold, peat moss, chopped sphagnum moss) to the potting mix, and give this plant lots of water.

Anthurium. This exotic-looking perennial is native to tropical America. Shiny, dark green leaves and large flower bracts in red, pink, and white look almost artificial. These plants like abundant humidity, high temperatures, and ample water. Plant in a potting mix of equal parts of leaf mold, sandy soil, and shredded osmunda.

(Continued on next page)

Aphelandra squarrosa. The foliage of this plant is quite outstanding; the dark green, waxy leaves have bold white veins. Flowers are large yellow clusters. Aphelandra needs high humidity and warm temperatures. You'll need to prune plants to keep them compact.

Begonia rex-cultorum. Commonly called the rex begonia, these house plants come in many varieties with magnificently patterned shieldlike leaves in colors of maroon, lilac, rose, greens, silvery gray, and combinations of these colors. These plants may go dormant in winter. They don't like to be overwatered or overfertilized. Plant them in a rich potting mix that's slightly acid (add peat moss, leaf mold, or other organic material to the mix).

Beloperone guttata. Its nickname is the shrimp plant because its tubular white, purple-spotted flowers are enclosed in coppery bronze overlapping bracts that resemble large shrimp. You will need to pinch and prune this plant constantly to keep it in shape. Place it in partial shade; too much sun may fade the foliage and bracts.

Caladium bicolor. Grown from tubers, caladium is native to tropical America. It has brightly colored, arrow-shaped, translucent leaves with splotches of red, pink, white, green, or silver; often a single leaf will show a variety of these colors. It likes high humidity and plenty of water. Foliage dies down in winter. Gradually withhold water, and in about a month, lift tubers and dry for 10 days. Store for the winter; repot the tubers in March.

Calathea. Related to the maranta (see next column), this striking foliage plant comes from tropical America. The foliage is beautifully marked in shades of green, white, and pink. It requires high humidity.

Cestrum. Grown for its showy, sometimes very fragrant flowers, this shrub is native to tropical America. It likes lots of water and humidity, warm temperatures, and sun about 4 hours a day. You will need to prune it to keep the plant compact.

Chamaeranthemum. This plant has foliage in different colors with veined patterns. It prefers high humidity and abundant water.

Clerodendrum thomsoniae. An evergreen vine from west Africa, clerodendrum has dark green, ribbed foliage and lanternlike white flowers that open to show red petals. You can train it on a support or use it in hanging baskets. It will need pruning.

Codiaeum. Commonly called croton, this tropical plant is grown for its leathery, glossy leaves in colors of green, yellow, red, purple, bronze, pink, or any combination of these. There are many leaf shapes. Plants like high humidity and plenty of water.

Coffea arabica. The coffee tree has glossy, dark green foliage and small, fragrant, white flowers that are followed by red berries. Each berry contains two coffee beans. You will need to pinch this plant to keep it under control.

Coleus blumei. The foliage of this plant can be velvety in texture, have ruffled or scalloped edges, and come in colors of green, chartreuse, yellow, salmon, peach, orange, red, magenta, purple, or brown. Several of these colors may appear on one leaf. The plant needs good, balanced light for best color. Pinch it frequently to keep a compact shape.

Colocasia esculenta. A large perennial with tuberous roots, this plant comes from tropical Asia and Polynesia. It has mammoth, heart-shaped, gray green leaves.

Cordyline terminalis. An evergreen, palmlike shrub, this plant has long bladelike leaves, usually with a variegation of purple or pink. It likes warm temperatures and high humidity.

Costus igneus. Called spiral ginger, this native of tropical America has smooth, glossy leaves arranged spirally on the stems. This plant can become quite large.

Crossandra infundibuliformis. This evergreen plant, native to India, has gardenialike foliage and showy flowers in scarlet orange or coral orange during the summer. The root ball should never dry out completely.

Ctenanthe. Related to maranta, this plant is grown for its unusual foliage, which may be on short or long stalks on the same plant. It produces insignificant white flowers.

Cyperus. This rushlike plant is related to the papyrus and has an umbrella-shaped cluster of leaves atop slender stems. It needs constant moisture; a good method of growing it is to submerge its roots in water. Divide the clumps when the plant becomes too large.

Ficus. This large, varied group of plants comes in many popular shapes. Most common are *F. elastica*, the rubber tree, and *F. benjamina*, the weeping fig. The weeping fig is most commonly grown as an indoor tree.

Fittonia verschaffeltii. Called the nerve plant because its white or pink veins are contrasted to the rest of the foliage, this creeping plant comes from South America. Never let the potting mix dry out.

Geogenanthus undatus. The leaves on this plant have a seersuckerlike texture. They are silvery green with white stripes and are purple underneath. Prune this plant often to keep it compact.

Hoya. This plant has thick, waxy foliage and tight clusters of small, waxy, star-shaped flowers. Give it some support to climb. It may go semidormant during the winter; let the potting mix dry out between waterings. Keep the plants potbound for best bloom.

Mandevilla 'Alice du Pont'. Also called dipladenia, this evergreen vine needs support to climb, or it can be trained in a hanging basket. It has glossy, dark green foliage and pink flowers from April through November. Pinch and prune this plant to keep it under control.

Maranta leuconeura. This foliage plant from tropical America is nicknamed the prayer plant because its leaves fold up at night, resembling praying hands. It has large green leaves with paired brown spots along the midrib. Prune out old or scraggly leaves.

Monstera deliciosa. Commonly called the split-leaf philodendron, this vine from tropical America has large, leathery, dark green leaves that are deeply cut and perforated. It needs good support to climb. The aerial roots it produces can be cut off without damage to the plant. Mature plants may produce callalike flowers which, if conditions are perfect, will develop into edible fruit.

Musa. The banana tree is a tender perennial that may grow in clumps. The dwarf forms are best to grow indoors. Musa has large, shiny leaves and, if conditions are just right, it may develop edible fruit. Plant in equal parts of potting mix and peat moss.

Nertera granadensis. This succulentlike plant has tiny, smooth, rounded leaves that look like small beads. It may produce small green flowers followed by bright orange, beadlike fruit. This plant needs constant moisture.

Passiflora. This plant is called the passion vine because its flowers symbolize elements of the Passion of Christ: the lacy crown could be a halo; the five stamens, the five wounds; the 10 petallike parts, the 10 faithful apostles. You will need to provide some support for it to climb; prune frequently.

Pilea. A large variety of juicy-stemmed plants with inconspicuous flowers, this family group is a popular one for growing indoors. Let the potting mix dry out between waterings.

Plectranthus. This vine, called Swedish ivy and creeping Charlie, makes an excellent hanging basket plant. Native to Africa, it has round, thick, almost succulent leaves. Tiny white flowers bloom on upright stems. It is fast-growing.

Polyscias. Related to the aralia family and native to tropical Asia and Polynesia, these interesting plants are generally touchy and are sensitive to cold and drafts. They prefer warmer temperatures and high humidity.

Stephanotis floribunda. Grown for its very fragrant, white, waxy flowers, this evergreen vine is a native of Malagasy. Its leaves are waxy and dark green, and it will need some support to climb.

Strelitzia reginae. The flowers of this plant are orange, blue, and white and resemble tropical birds—hence its nickname, bird of paradise. A tropical perennial, it blooms throughout the year. Give it generous amounts of fertilizer for best bloom.

Garden room *shares space with dining area. Plants lend pleasant atmosphere to entertaining; smaller ones join diners at table.*

Entryway to house, *covered with corrugated fiberglass over 2 by 4 beams, protects collection of tropical plants growing in ground. Vining plants are trained against house wall. Brick walkway can be cleaned with hose.*

If pests and diseases invade

One day you may suddenly notice that a serpent has entered your Garden of Eden...your prized plants are covered with horrid crawling creatures, or a crippling disease has disfigured some beautiful foliage or perfect blossoms. What can you do?

Happily, many of these problems can be quickly eradicated. By improving a few gardening habits and doing some needed pruning, you can restore your greenhouse to its former glory.

Preventive medicine

The greenhouse environment that is so perfect for growing plants has one flaw: it's also the perfect environment for many of the pests and diseases that attack plants. If left unchecked, these pests and diseases could quickly decimate an entire greenhouse population. But there are many steps you can take to keep things under control.

Though no plant is completely immune to pests or diseases, you can lessen the risks by taking a few simple precautions. Many of the following preventive measures are mentioned elsewhere in this book, but they bear repeating.

1) Use clean plant containers and sterilized potting mixes whenever you plant or transplant greenhouse specimens.

2) Examine all new plants carefully before introducing them into the greenhouse environment. If they are carrying pests or diseases, they could cause an epidemic.

3) Familiarize yourself with every new plant you bring into your greenhouse so you'll know whether or not you're providing for its growing requirements. Try to meet each plant's needs as closely as possible. Pests and diseases are less likely to strike a healthy, happy plant.

4) Check over all your plants periodically (this can be very time-consuming if you have a large greenhouse, but it's well worth your effort). Look at them carefully to see if they're healthy and if they need repotting. This inspection should ferret out any plant that has a problem.

5) If you do find a pest-infested or diseased plant, get it out of the greenhouse—now! Cure it if you can, but if it is beyond your help, harden your heart and discard it.

A rogue's gallery of pests

Most pests that invade your greenhouse are small, almost microscopic, insects. You may not be aware of the little creatures until your favorite plant takes a turn for the worse. When you do find pests, get rid of them as quickly as possible.

There are two approaches to pest control: one is a direct method, involving physical removal of the pests; the other requires using pesticides, a less direct method that could harm your plant.

The direct approach is to remove pests by hand or to wash them off the plants with water from a hose or a mist sprayer. One advantage to this approach is that it can be repeated as often as needed to control pests. Most insecticides require a certain waiting period between applications. The main problem with this approach is that you might be unable to eliminate insect eggs in the soil.

Spraying delicate plants with insecticides can be almost as harmful to some plants as the pest infestation itself.

Fuzzy, white mealybugs *hide on undersides of leaves at joint; can ruin plant if not quickly eradicated.*

Aphids cluster *on hibiscus flower bud, sucking out plant juices. Uncontrolled, these pests ruin flowers or leave plant with curled, distorted leaves. Heavy infestation can even stunt plant growth.*

Chameleons – the natural pest killers –

Though the greenhouse environment encourages harmful insect buildups, it's possible for your plants to be pest-free without being sprayed with pesticides. The ecological answer to your greenhouse insect problems could be chameleons, which keep insect populations checked without weakening plants as sprays can.

Chameleons are small (about 3 inches long), shy lizards that have the ability to change body color. Since they're native to tropical areas such as the southeastern United States, the Caribbean, Mexico, and Central and South America, they do best at about 80°. Chameleons have proved to be excellent insect controllers in greenhouses, which are suitable homes since they're warm and humid.

For the average home greenhouse, you'll probably need about four to six chameleons; they are available at most pet stores. Plan to have one lizard for every 12 to 15 square feet of ground area; adjust the figure upward or downward if you have a particularly large or small number of plants for the size of the house. Remember that if you get too many chameleons, some may starve.

When the chameleons are first released it would be wise to put out some food—mealworms or crickets—to tide them over while they get used to their new home; this usually takes about a week. Another thing to remember is that these lizards can't drink water out of a dish. They get their liquid from condensation on the foliage—so mist daily; it's good for the plants, too.

Even if you think you have a pest-free greenhouse, your chameleons will probably thrive; they eat insects you can't even see.

Don't be alarmed if you can't find your chameleons. It's likely the shy little fellows are still there, hidden among the plants. Take precautions to keep them contained, though. Don't leave the door open, and cover the vents with small-grid window screens.

Put those chemical sprays away (they could be fatal to your chameleons) and give these insect lovers a try. Some day, when you least expect it, you'll probably pick up a pest-free plant and see a well-fed chameleon staring at you.

Chameleon waits *on orchid flower stalk for unsuspecting insect.*

Always read and carefully follow label directions on pesticides. Be sure the insecticide is intended to eliminate the specific pest attacking your plant and that it is recommended for use on that particular plant. Some tender plants, such as ferns, may succumb to the spray itself. It's best to spray plants outdoors, where any residue will be dispersed in the open air and you can be sure to cover all the leaf surfaces, both top and bottom.

By acquainting yourself with the pests that frequent greenhouses, you should be able to identify and eradicate any pest you find. The description of each pest includes the suggested methods of disposing of it efficiently.

Aphids. These pests have soft, round or pear-shaped bodies, usually green, reddish, or black. They may have wings. They tend to cluster in groups on flower buds or on new plant growth (see photo on page 92, bottom right). They suck plant juices from the stems and leaves, causing poor growth or curled, distorted leaves or flowers. In addition, they attract ants with their honeydew secretions, which can also form a base for a sooty mold. Wash the aphids off with a forceful stream of water or use pyrethrum or rotenone.

Ants. These familiar crawling insects are usually red or black. Some kinds protect aphids or mealybugs and feed on the honeydew. The ants' nests may injure plant roots. They don't damage plants directly, but they encourage other plant pests that do. Kill them by hand or use malathion spray.

Earwigs. Crawling insects, earwigs have long, brownish bodies with long pincers protruding from their tails. They are night-feeding pests that chew leaves and flowers. You will need to check damaged plants at night to identify this culprit. Remove them from plants by hand or spray them with malathion.

Leafhoppers. These small, fast-moving, green or brownish insects suck plant juices from stems and leaves. By feeding on the underside of leaves, they cause a white stippling visible on the upper side. Some types of leafhoppers can spread virus diseases. Wash them off plants or spray them with pyrethrum or rotenone.

Mealybugs. Though large enough to be spotted easily, these sneaky pests normally cluster on leaf stems or in branch crotches out of the light—a habit that makes them difficult to spot. They have round, white, fuzzy-looking bodies. They are pictured on page 92, top right. Mealybugs cause stunted plant growth, and they secrete honeydew, which attracts ants and forms a base where sooty mold can grow. Remove them by hand, touch them with a cotton swab that has been dipped in alcohol, or spray them with petroleum oils.

Scale insects. Scale exists in many varieties. Usually brown or gray with a round or oval body, scale insects have a hard shell covering in their adult stage. Some types attack plant leaves; others attack stems. They can be especially hard to detect on ferns, as they resemble spores. Scale insects are pictured on page 94 at top left. These insects suck plant juices, causing stunted or poor plant growth. They also secrete a honeydew that gives leaves a shiny, sticky surface and attracts ants. You can scrape scale insects off with your fingernail or a small knife, swab them with a soapy solution (don't use detergent), or use lime sulfur or petroleum oils as directed on their labels. You can also spray with nicotine sulfate.

Snails and slugs. The bane of many gardeners, snails and slugs are among the commonest, most destructive of all greenhouse pests. They feed at night and on cool, overcast days. You can identify their damage because they leave a trail of silvery slime. The best way to deal with these beasts is to bait them with metaldehyde. It comes in meal or pellet form and actually attracts them. Place the bait in a dish or paper plate under a bench or near the door; snails and slugs often die on the spot, so you can discard them with the plate. Metaldehyde mixed with bran isn't harmful to birds or pets. Other types of bait should be kept out of reach.

Spider mites. Minute pests, spider mites are detectable only in groups or by the characteristic webbing they leave on

Scale insects *are flat and roundish, latch onto undersides of plant leaves, stems. This plant shows heavy infestation.*

Spider mites' web *completely encases marigold flower bud. Mites are minute; infestation is characterized by fine webbing, yellow-mottled foliage, or white stippling on leaves.*

plant foliage. Mites have flat, oval bodies, usually white or red (see the photograph at bottom left). Plant damage may cause leaves to turn yellow and die, or the foliage may become mottled with brown or yellow spots. Silvery stippling and an overall grayish look also indicate mites. Infested plants will be stunted and may die. When you find an infested plant, isolate it at once, for these creatures spread rapidly. Wash them off with water or a soapy solution, use lime sulfur or petroleum oils, or spray with ryania.

Thrips. Very small and fast-moving, thrips are barely visible to the eye. They have slender bodies in colors of tan, brown, or black, with lighter-colored markings. If you disturb them, they fly or leap. Thrips feed on foliage or flowers, causing distortion of leaves, and buds that don't open. Their rasping damage is sometimes noticeable on stems or leaf edges. Wash them off with water or apply pyrethrum, rotenone, or petroleum oils.

Whiteflies. These common pests are very small, white, flying insects. They flutter about plants in a white cloud when you disturb them. The larvae resemble scale insects and cling to the undersides of plant leaves. Attacked foliage turns a pale color, and the leaf surface is covered with a shiny, sticky layer of honeydew that attracts ants and may invite sooty mold to invade. You can wash whiteflies off with water or use pyrethrum, rotenone, or petroleum oils. Whiteflies are very persistent and may require several applications.

Dealing with diseases

Many diseases can be avoided if you practice good gardening techniques. This involves keeping your greenhouse clear of weeds, dead flowers, or fallen leaves. Remove any plants that appear to be pest-infested or diseased. Remove annuals and vegetables growing in beds or under benches as soon as their normal season is past. Old and weak plants are especially susceptible to disease.

A few of the common diseases that strike greenhouse plants are listed here with suggested solutions for controlling each problem.

Black spot. Black spots appear on the foliage of diseased plants. The best method of keeping this problem under control is to discard the diseased plant.

Crown or root rot. Plants infected will turn brown and mushy or suddenly collapse. This problem is usually caused by poor drainage or overwatering. If you catch it in time, you may be able to save the plant by repotting it; otherwise, discard it. Correcting your watering habits is the only known control for this disease.

Damping off. Newly sprouted seedlings develop a stem rot near the soil surface and fall over, or the seeds never sprout at all. The only way to prevent this is to clean your flats and containers before reusing them and use only sterilized soil mixes.

Powdery mildew. This appears as a bluish white dust that covers leaves, stems, and flower buds. Foliage may curl or be distorted. The main causes are overwatering and poor air circulation. Try moving the infected plants to a better location, removing the damaged portions of the plant, or spraying with sulfur dust or benomyl. A badly infected plant should be discarded.

Rust. Blisters form on infected plant leaves and scatter reddish or yellow spores. Remove the infected leaves.

A list of greenhouse manufacturers

If you decide to buy a greenhouse, you will want to see just what's available and compare the various models before you make your purchase. The following list includes some of the larger greenhouse manufacturers; most of them will also supply the various systems for climate control. You can contact them directly for catalogues, price lists, and other information.

Another good source is the Yellow Pages of your telephone directory; look under "Greenhouse Builders" and "Greenhouse Equipment & Supplies."

Aluminum Greenhouses, Inc.
14615 Lorain Avenue
Cleveland, OH 44111

BACO Leisure Products, Inc.
19 East 47th Street
New York, NY 10017

W. Atlee Burpee Company
5556 Burpee Building
Warminster, PA 18974

Cap-N-Nail Mfg. Co.
625 Poinsettia Street
Santa Ana, CA 92701

Casaplanta
9489 Dayton Way
Beverly Hills, CA 90210

Columbia Gorge Rehabilitation Center
Route 1, Box 705
Hood River, OR 97031

Continental Greenhouse Distributors
3471 Peachtree Road, NE
Atlanta, GA 30326

Creative Living
Dept. 102-AZ
2627 Hillegass
Berkeley, CA 94704

Fremont Greenhouses
P. O. Box 2397
Dublin, CA 94566

Gardendome Greenhouses
P. O. Box 1239
Corvallis, OR 97330

Gothic Arch Greenhouses
P. O. Box 1564
Mobile, AL 36601

The Greenery
P. O. Box 489
Soquel, CA 95073

Peter Reimuller
The Greenhouseman
980 Seventeenth Avenue
Santa Cruz, CA 95063

Janco Greenhouses
Box 348
Beltsville, MD 20705

Lord & Burnham
2 Main Street
Irvington, NY 10533

McGregor Greenhouses
Box 36
Santa Cruz, CA 95063

Monterey Greenhouses
P. O. Box 806
Freedom, CA 95019

Pacific Coast Greenhouse Mfg. Co.
430 Hurlingame Avenue
Redwood City, CA 94063

Redfern Greenhouses
57 Mount Hermon Road
Scotts Valley, CA 95066

Redwood Domes
P. O. Box 666
Aptos, CA 95003

Santa Barbara Greenhouses
2675½ Daily Drive
Camarillo, CA 93010

Sturdi-Built Manufacturing Co.
11304 SW Boones Ferry Road
Portland, OR 97219

Terra-Phernalia
Earth Oriented Imports
P. O. Box 504
Millbrae, CA 94030

Texas Greenhouses Co. Inc.
2723 St. Louis Avenue
Fort Worth, TX 76110

Vis Vita Solarium
P. O. Box 9020
Seattle, WA 98109

H. Wolff Manufacturing Co.
955 Celia Way
Palo Alto, CA 94303

Photographers

William Aplin: 16 (all), 45 (top right), 55, 78. **Peter W. Behn:** 22 (top). **Mary Kay Bernitt:** 47 (lower right). **Lorraine Marshall Burgess:** 66 (top). **Glenn M. Christiansen:** 11 (center right), 22 (lower), 23 (lower), 41 (top right), 49 (lower), 70, 85 (center). **Gordon W. Dillon:** 67 (left). **Annelise Dunmire:** 60 (lower right). **Gerald R. Fredrick:** 37 (lower left), 49 (top). **Lenore Hedla:** 89 (left). **Peggy Kuhn:** 93. **Longwood Gardens:** 5 (left, top right). **Ells Marugg:** 4, 6, 10 (lower), 11 (top), 13 (top, center), 15 (all), 17 (all), 18 (all), 20, 21 (top), 25 (all), 26 (all), 27 (all), 28 (left), 29 (all), 31 (all), 33 (right), 35 (left), 39 (all), 40, 41 (top left, center, lower left), 44 (lower), 45 (lower right), 46 (all), 54, 57 (top), 60 (top, lower left), 61 (top), 71 (lower left), 74, 75 (right), 76 (top), 83 (top), 85 (top, lower), 86 (lower), 92 (lower), 94 (lower). **Don Normark:** 11 (center left, lower left, lower right), 12 (all), 13 (lower left, lower right), 19 (all), 21 (lower left, lower right), 23 (top), 28 (right), 36, 37 (top, lower right), 38, 41 (lower left), 47 (top left, top right, lower left), 59 (all), 72, 73 (all), 75 (left), 76 (lower), 84, 86 (top left, top right), 88, 89 (right), 91 (top). **Norman A. Plate:** 45 (top left), 61 (lower left), 79, 83 (lower), 91 (lower), 92 (top), 94 (top). **Donald W. Vandervort:** 5 (lower right). **Darrow M. Watt:** 10 (top), 33 (left), 34 (all), 35 (center, right), 43, 44 (top), 45 (center left, center right), 48 (all), 49 (center), 57 (lower), 61 (lower center, lower right), 65, 66 (lower), 67 (right), 68, 71 (top, lower right). **Peter O. Whiteley:** 50, 53, 87. **Doug Wilson:** 56 (left), 82. **Joyce R. Wilson:** 64 (all). **George Woo:** 45 (lower left), 56 (right).

Index